This Ju 88R-1 of NJG 3 defected to RAF Dyce, Scotland, on May 9, 1943. It is seen here following its arrival and removal of the radar aerials (RAF Museum)

A Ju 88A-1 of KG 51 'Edelweiß' is scene undergoing investigation, possibly at Farnborough, in 1940. (Key Collection)

Oblt Mathias Schwegler was a pilot with KG 51, and the first in that unit to receive the Ritterkreuz. When war began he was with Stab III./KG 51, then I./KG 51. Shot down over Russia on July 11, 1941, he and his crew returned and later he commanded 12./KG 51. Schwegler died on April 18, 1945 in unknown circumstances. (Chris Goss)

FOREWORD

Versatile, successful, and generally revered by its crews, the Ju 88 was truly a star among frontline combat aircraft flown by Germany's Luftwaffe during World War Two. Built in large numbers (around 15,000) in a wide variety of different versions, it ably fulfilled several vital frontline roles during that conflict. The type is therefore unquestionably a fitting subject for this, the third volume in Key Publishing's successful Combat Machines series.

Conceived originally as a 'schnellbomber' or fast light/medium bomber (a role it performed during much of World War Two), Junkers' Ju 88 progressed effortlessly into other demanding mission profiles.

It became a heavy fighter, destroyer, ground-attack and close-support aircraft, radar-equipped night fighter, conversion trainer, and a long-range reconnaissance asset… and was the basis of a closely related development, the Ju 188. This ubiquitous twin was active on all fronts, in war-torn skies as far flung as Western Europe, the Soviet Union and North Africa. Britain's equally superlative de Havilland Mosquito alone matched the Ju 88 as such a versatile 'maid of all work'.

The Ju 88 has long been popular among modellers, too, and there has been a veritable profusion of kits, aftermarket accessories and decals available over the years…and they are still being released. The most recent offerings are the 1/48 'glass-nosed' Ju 88s from Ukraine's ICM, but the firm is also planning a gun-nosed C-6 to boost the range. It has been my pleasure to research this aircraft type over many years, and it's always been fascinating. I hope this book will appeal to both modellers and aviation enthusiasts alike as an entry-level guide to the type, via a wide selection of period imagery, detailed text (some of which corrects erroneous data published elsewhere), high-quality colour artwork, a cutaway drawing and exclusive walk-around images.

Malcolm V Lowe
Author

Author: Malcolm V Lowe
Series Editor: Chris Clifford
Acknowledgements: The author gratefully acknowledges the assistance of the following with the provision of information and images: John Batchelor MBE, Martin Hale, John Levesley, Jim Smith, Andy Sweet, Csaba Bordács (Hungary,) Hans Meier and Peter Walter (Germany,) Nikolay Baranov (Russia)

Assistant Editor: Stu Fone
Group Editor: Nigel Price
Colour artwork: Andy Hay – Flying Art
Designer: Tom Bagley
Group Designer: Steve Donovan
Production Manager: Janet Watkins
Commercial Director: Ann Saundry
Managing Director: Adrian Cox
Executive Chairman: Richard Cox

Key Publishing Ltd: PO Box 100, Stamford, Lincolnshire, PE9 1XQ, United Kingdom.

Distributed by: Seymour Distribution Ltd, 2 Poultry Avenue, London, EC1A 9PP. Tel: 020 7429 4000. Fax: 020 7429 4001.
Printed by: Warners (Midland) plc, Bourne.
Printed in England
ISBN: 9781912205325

STOLEN DYNASTY

The giant G 38 airliner of 1929-30 was an attempt by Junkers to break into the developing (and large) commercial aircraft market. It could seat up to 34 passengers, including several in the wing centre section. (via Hans Meier)

Creator and manufacturer of the Ju 88, the Junkers organisation was, in its day, one of the world's most important aviation companies

One of the iconic names in aviation history is the German aircraft manufacturer Junkers.

Created by Hugo Junkers before World War One, the company was a pioneer in the establishment of metal as a primary material in airframe construction, and was a world-leader in the introduction and development of all-metal aircraft structures. Today, the widespread use of metal in aircraft manufacturing is taken for granted, but in the World War One era this was truly cutting-edge technology. Junkers went on to become one of the world's largest aviation firms during its existence up to 1945, and became a major supplier of warplanes to Nazi Germany's Luftwaffe.

The inspiration for the pioneering and vitally important introduction of all-metal aircraft into mainstream acceptance was Hugo Junkers himself. Born during February 1859 in Rheydt, near latter-day Mönchengladbach (ironically the area from where the arch-Nazi Joseph Goebbels also hailed), Junkers initially studied engineering and thermodynamics. A talented and pragmatic engineer, he eventually held several thermodynamic and metallurgical patents, and during the mid-1890s, he created his own business, Junkers und Compagnie in Dessau, specialising in metal-working and making a range of appliances, including gas-fired boilers and heaters. Dessau was a comparatively small but nonetheless important town, in what is now the eastern part of present-day Germany. Additionally, during the 1890s he gained a Professorship of mechanical engineering at what became the Royal Technical University at Aachen.

The original Junkers all-metal aircraft was the J 1 of 1915... an advanced cantilever mid-wing monoplane sometimes branded the 'Tin Donkey'. (Junkers)

Pioneering work

Like so many engineers of his generation, Professor Junkers became fascinated by the new and developing science of manned powered flight, which the Wright Brothers in the US did so much to pioneer. While at Aachen he joined forces with Professor Hans Reissner, whose interest in and enthusiasm for aeronautical innovations led to several important developments from 1908 to 1910. These culminated with the granting to Hugo Junkers of a highly significant patent (Patentschrift Nr. 253788), dated February 1, 1910, and issued by Imperial Germany's Kaiserliches Patentamt. This was for an all-metal cantilever wing design with a unique airfoil configuration. Although it was somewhat eccentric, in proposing to fit those on board within the actual airfoil shape as a virtual flying wing, Junkers' patent was nevertheless ground-breaking. It was the first time that such an all-metal design for an

aircraft structure had been proposed and thought through sufficiently to warrant the granting of a patent.

This placed Junkers far ahead of the then-current aeronautical design philosophy of using fabric-covered wooden structures with external struts and bracing (rigging). With his company already able to work with metal in the fabrication of domestic and engineering appliances it had been established to manufacture, Junkers was in a unique position to put his

theories into practical reality. The first attempt at making a viable metal aircraft was achieved in co-operation with Reissner, the resulting canard design flying during 1912.

World War One prompted the widespread use of aviation for the first time in a major conflict, and many companies involved in aviation activities came to the forefront. Junkers was well placed with its extensive experience of metal-working to begin making aircraft ➤➤

Junkers gained great success and considerable fame with the ground-breaking F 13 all-metal passenger aircraft. This civil-registered example of 'Dobrolet' was photographed in the Soviet Union (via Nikolay Baranov)

A peaceful pre-war view of the Junkers factory and airfield at Dessau. Various Junkers aircraft types can be seen parked on the airfield, including several Ju 52/3m transports. (John Batchelor Collection)

along the lines proposed by Hugo Junkers himself. Junkers was convinced the way forward for aircraft design and manufacture was with metal rather than wooden airframes. He joined forces with two talented engineers, Otto Reuter and Otto Mader, and the result was a succession of aircraft designs that established the Junkers pedigree in the use of metal for aircraft construction.

The original Junkers metal aircraft was the J 1 of 1915. This has sometimes been called the 'Blechesel' (variously translated as 'Tin Donkey' or 'Sheet-metal Donkey'). It is generally believed to have first flown on December 12, 1915, and has been widely regarded as the world's first practical all-metal aircraft. Its streamlined metal un-braced layout was very different to the warplanes at that time, in action with their wooden structures and major external bracing. Nevertheless, the J 1 was more of a demonstrator than a serious production prototype; its construction contained steel, making it too heavy to be a practical combat aircraft.

During late 1916 the Idflieg (the 'Inspektion der Fliegertruppen' or Inspectorate of Flying or Aviation Troops…Imperial Germany's organisation that oversaw German military aviation) announced a J-type design specification for an armoured ground-attack, observation and army co-operation aircraft. Junkers responded with one of the most revolutionary aircraft of the war, the Junkers J 4. The first prototype/development example flew on January 28, 1917, and with the official designation J.I the type entered service during July 1917 with units of the Deutsche Luftstreitkräfte (Imperial Germany's air service). Its lighter yet still robust all-metal duralumin (aluminium) construction, including corrugated skinning, made it strong and difficult to shoot down.

Approximately 225 or 227 examples of the J 4 were built, and they became part of a line of metal aircraft that Junkers designed during the war. However, Junkers' ponderous manufacturing practices at that time were too slow for the Idflieg. This resulted in a short and temperamental relationship from 1917, with none other than Dutchman Anthony Fokker, whose aviation manufacturing capabilities were far more prolific than those of Junkers. Apart from the

J 4, the next most important Junkers aircraft of that time was the all-metal J 9 fighter, which again featured corrugated metal skinning and served in small numbers as the Junkers D.I before the war ended.

Inter-war success

Unlike many German aviation companies that suffered under the terms of the peace agreements made after the end of World War One, Junkers actually began to thrive. A new company, Junkers Flugzeugwerke AG, was established at Dessau during April 1919. The basic layout and construction techniques of the Junkers military all-metal aircraft of the war years were redirected into the growing field of civil aviation, and for the following 15 or so years Junkers became one of the world's chief civil aircraft manufacturers. Vital to this success was the Junkers F 13, generally regarded as the world's first viable all-metal transport aircraft. The single-engined corrugated-skinned F 13 first flew on June 25, 1919. The type was a great success and was exported widely, a total of 322 examples being built. Able to seat four passengers comfortably, the type proved useful on many developing internal and short-range airline routes, and some examples were used for pioneering flights in different parts of the world, for which their rugged construction was well suited.

The Junkers company also had an engine design and manufacturing facility which, during 1923, became a separate entity; its products

were usually referred to with the abbreviation 'Jumo'. It went on to create modern and powerful inline engines suitable for military aviation such as the Jumo 210 and 211.

Russian adventure

Several Junkers inter-war types were licence-built successfully in Sweden.

Far less profitable, though, was an unlikely and ultimately unsuccessful partnership with the Soviet Union. A Junkers offshoot was established at Fili just outside Moscow in the early 1920s, but this collaboration with Russian industry eventually ended acrimoniously. The chief beneficiaries were the Soviet authorities. Russian industry gained a considerable amount of information from Junkers' activities at Fili, including the use of all-metal structures for aircraft design

and manufacture, and the means to fabricate the all-important sheet metal itself.

Forced take-over

Junkers' enduring success as a commercial aircraft producer following World War One was largely thanks to the iconic F 13 airliner and the type was followed by a succession of all-metal transports during the 1920s and early 1930s, which established the Junkers brand. Important among these were the tri-motor G 24 series, the single-engined W 33 and W 34, and eventually the best-known of them all, the three-engined Junkers Ju 52/3m. The latter first flew as a tri-motor (the layout was originally single-engined) during March 1932, but by then problems were developing in Germany. ⏩

Junkers' Ju 90 airliner was based on the cancelled Ju 89 long-range bomber programme, which had effectively ended with General Wever's death during 1936. The related Ju 290 later partnered Ju 88s used for maritime missions. (Malcolm V Lowe Collection)

Pre-dating the Ju 88, but designed to different parameters, was the Ju 86 twin-engined bomber. This lumbering machine was out of service as a major bomber type for the Luftwaffe by World War Two, but Germany's ally, Hungary operated several examples as shown here. (Fortepan, Hungary)

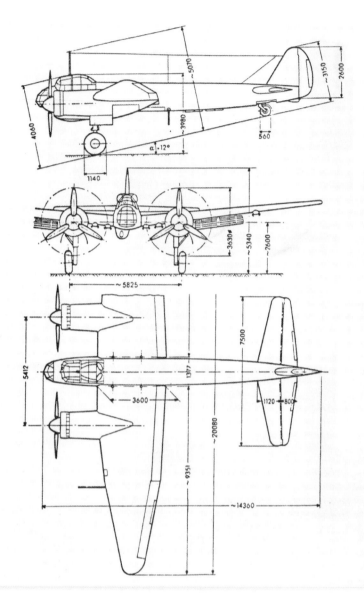

was Dr Heinrich Koppenberg. A sympathetic supporter who had become important in the ranks of the Nazi hierarchy, Koppenberg at once set about remaking Junkers in the Nazi image, gearing the company to producing warplanes to suit the foreign policy ambitions of the new German leadership. The Junkers aviation and engine companies were subsequently amalgamated during 1936 under a new organisation, Junkers Flugzeug und Motorenwerke AG.

A succession of major types followed, which were to play such a significant influence on Germany's war-making capabilities during the coming years. Chief among these were the iconic Junkers Ju 87 Stuka dive-bomber and the equally important and far more prolific Ju 88 series. Other types such as the Ju 86, Ju 90 and Ju 290 all contributed in one way or another to Nazi Germany's war machine.

By the latter stages of World War Two, the Junkers organisation had grown into a massive enterprise. In addition to the parent plant there were related manufacturing locations spread across Germany, which were either a part of Junkers, or related to it within the Nazi German aircraft industry's manufacturing system. Post-war Allied intelligence analysis of the company's activities identified that approximately up to 140,000 people

The Ju 87 Stuka dive-bomber was the most well-known and arguably the most notorious of Junkers' products. It was a major success in the early part of World War Two as a part of the German 'Blitzkrieg', and was sold under export to countries such as Italy, the operator of this example. (Key Collection)

Within a year, during January 1933, Hitler's Nazis gained power in Germany and everything subsequently changed for Junkers. Just a few months later the company had been seized and completely taken over by the Nazis. They were unable or unwilling to work with Hugo Junkers, who they considered to be a socialist pacifist and therefore likely to be unwilling to comply with their plans. Desperate to become the owners of his various patents, which had multiplied to cover various technologies used in existing Junkers designs, the Nazis simply seized control. Hugo Junkers himself was placed under house arrest and eventually forced to relinquish control of not only his company, but his cherished patents as well. As a result, he died on his 76th birthday during February 1935.

A central figure in the reorganisation of Junkers following Nazi seizure

Ju 88 Specifications (Junkers Ju 88A-4)

Wingspan	65ft 10½in (20.08m)
Length	47ft 1.25in (14.36m)
Height	16ft 7.5in (5.07m) (to tip of radio mast, tail on ground)
Maximum speed	292mph (470km/h) at 17,388ft (5,300m)
Maximum take-off weight	30,865lb (14,000kg)
Maximum range	approximately 1,510 miles (2,430km)
Service ceiling	29,500ft (9,000m) without external load
Armament	Three (typical) MG 81 7.92mm machine guns, in various factory-made flexible-mounted locations, and twin MG 81Z unit in lower C-Stand location; extra armament often added such as two additional MG 15 7.92mm in side windows; up to 7,936lb (3,600kg) of bombs for short-range missions, common 4,409lb (2,000kg)
Engine	Two Junkers Jumo 211J liquid-cooled inverted V12 inline engines, of 1,401hp (1,044kW) each at 2,600rpm take-off power at sea level
Crew	Four (pilot; bomb-aimer/front gunner; radio operator/rear gunner; navigator/ventral gunner – all four had machine gun defensive armament at or near to their work stations)

Note: The metric data listed here represent actual measurements adhered to by Junkers, and are quoted on the company's factory drawings and other Ju 88 documentation. The Imperial measurements are conversions from those original metric measurements, not the other way around. Some published sources quote the Ju 88A-4's length as being almost 47ft 3in, but this is not an accurate equivalent of the true dimension of 14.36m.

A Ju 88 sails serenely above the clouds in this evocative image. The type was one of the most important warplanes for the Luftwaffe during World War Two, and served in a multitude of roles. (Malcolm V Lowe Collection)

were involved in Junkers design, construction and related activities during 1945.

At that time, Junkers' designers had various advanced ideas on their drawing boards, but the turn of events in world history was to result in some of these projects reappearing in the post-war Soviet Union, following the final defeat of Nazi Germany. Dessau itself was captured by US forces, and not those of the Soviet Union, during April 1945 shortly before the end of the war in Europe. However, under agreements reached at the highest levels regarding the future map of Europe following the defeat of the Nazis, that part of Germany was situated in the area that later came under Soviet influence, being on the wrong side of the Iron Curtain in what became East Germany.

Ironically this began a second period of connection between Junkers and the Russians. Although the Americans are claimed to have taken everything from Junkers' Dessau facilities, the truth was more complicated. Russian technicians who duly visited Junkers' facilities at Dessau gained much

valuable material, and successfully rounded up a number of company employees who were transported to the Soviet Union without delay.

As in the 1920s, once more the Russians benefited directly from this – generally unwilling – transfer of ideas and techniques from Junkers. One of the results was the resurrection by the Soviets of a major late-war Junkers design, the futuristic forward-swept wing Ju 287 jet-powered bomber. Also called the EF 131 and later OKB-1, the machine was flown briefly in the Soviet Union but did not enter

service. Nevertheless, the lessons gained by the Russians from former Junkers employees such as Brunolf Baade, who also became important in East Germany's Cold War aircraft industry, were of great significance.

The name Junkers itself survived following the war, albeit in Cold War West Germany. A shadow of its former self, the Junkers that emerged from the defeat of Nazi Germany was simply Junkers GmbH, and this was eventually merged into the major Messerschmitt-Bölkow-Blohm (MBB) consortium of the late 1960s. ▪

GLOSSARY & TRANSLATIONS

Here's a handy guide to Luftwaffe and general World War Two technical terms

AG	Aktiengesellschaft (roughly equivalent to a joint-stock company)
ATG	Allgemeine Transportanlage GmbH (sometimes written as Allgemeine Transportanlage Gesellschaft mbH)
Bf	abbreviation for Messerschmitt aircraft; generally, the Bf 109 series was the last from this manufacturer to use this abbreviation, the company changing its name from BFW to Messerschmitt and so subsequently using 'Me'
BFW	Bayerische Flugzeugwerke AG, the original designer of the Bf 109 and other types such as the Bf 110
BMW	Bayerische Motorenwerke AG (sometimes also written Bayerische Motoren Werke AG)
cg	centre of gravity
C-in-C	Commander-in-Chief
c/n	construction number
DB	Daimler Benz (sometimes also written Daimler-Benz)
Dipl-Ing	Diplom-Ingenieur (literally a Diploma Engineer, roughly equivalent to an engineering Degree in a specific engineering subject)
EKdo	Erprobungskommando (Luftwaffe service trials/service evaluation centre)
E-Stelle	Erprobungsstelle (Luftwaffe trials and evaluation unit)
FuG	Funk Gerät (literally radio set or apparatus, the generic designation used for radio, radar, IFF, etc in the Ju 88, Bf 110, Bf 109, Fw 190 and other types)
Fw	Focke-Wulf Flugzeugbau GmbH
GmbH	Gesellschaft mit beschränkter Haftung (roughly equivalent to a British Limited Company)
GM	abbreviated designation for the GM 1 nitrous oxide (sometimes written as GM-1) used for boosting the power output of some German piston engines
Höhenjäger	high-altitude fighter
hp	horse power
IFF	Identification Friend/Foe
Jagdstaffel	fighter squadron
JG	Jagdgeschwader (Luftwaffe fighter wing)
Ju	Junkers (Junkers Flugzeug und Motorenwerke AG)
kg	kilogram
KG	Kampfgeschwader (Luftwaffe bomber wing)
KGr	Kampfgruppe (Luftwaffe bomber group)
LG	Lehrgeschwader (Luftwaffe 'teaching' wing, but actually combat wing)
Ltd	Limited Company (UK)
Me	abbreviation for Messerschmitt aircraft; generally the Bf 109 series was one of the last from this manufacturer to use this abbreviation, the company changing its name from BFW to Messerschmitt and so subsequently using 'Me' for types such as Me 209, Me 410, etc.
MW	abbreviated designation for the MW 50 methanol-water used for boosting the power output of some German piston engines
NASM	National Air and Space Museum (United States)
NSGr	Nachtschlachtgruppe (Luftwaffe night attack group)
NJG	Nachtjagdgeschwader (Luftwaffe night fighter wing)
ObdH	Oberbefehlshaber ders Heeres (Army C-in-C's office)
ObdL	Oberbefehlshaber der Luftwaffe (Luftwaffe C-in-C's office)
OKL	Oberkommando der Luftwaffe (Luftwaffe high command)
R	Rüstsatz (plural, Rüstsätze – not Rüstsätzen), the conversion kits or sets (often concerned with add-on armament options) for installation in the field
RAF	Royal Air Force
Reichsverteidigung	Reich defence fighter force
Revi	Reflexvisier (literally reflex gunsight, the generic designation for gunsights carried in some German military aircraft)
RLM	Reichsluftfahrtministerium, the Third Reich's aviation ministry
rpg	rounds per gun
rpm	revolutions per minute
s/n	serial number
Stab	headquarters
TA	Technisches Amt, the RLM's technical designs office
U	Umrüst-Bausatz (plural, Umrüst-Bausätze), the conversion kits or sets installed at the factory to give a particular equipment fit or capability
UK	United Kingdom
US	United States
USAAF	United States Army Air Force(s)
V	Versuchs or Versuchsmuster, the term used to describe an experimental or development/test airframe, not necessarily a prototype
VDM	Vereinigte Deutsche Metallwerke (Metawerke) AG, propeller manufacturer
VfH	Versuchsstelle für Höhenflüge
VHF	Very High Frequency (radio)
WNr	Werk Nummer (German construction number)
ZG	Zerstörergeschwader (Luftwaffe heavy fighter wing)

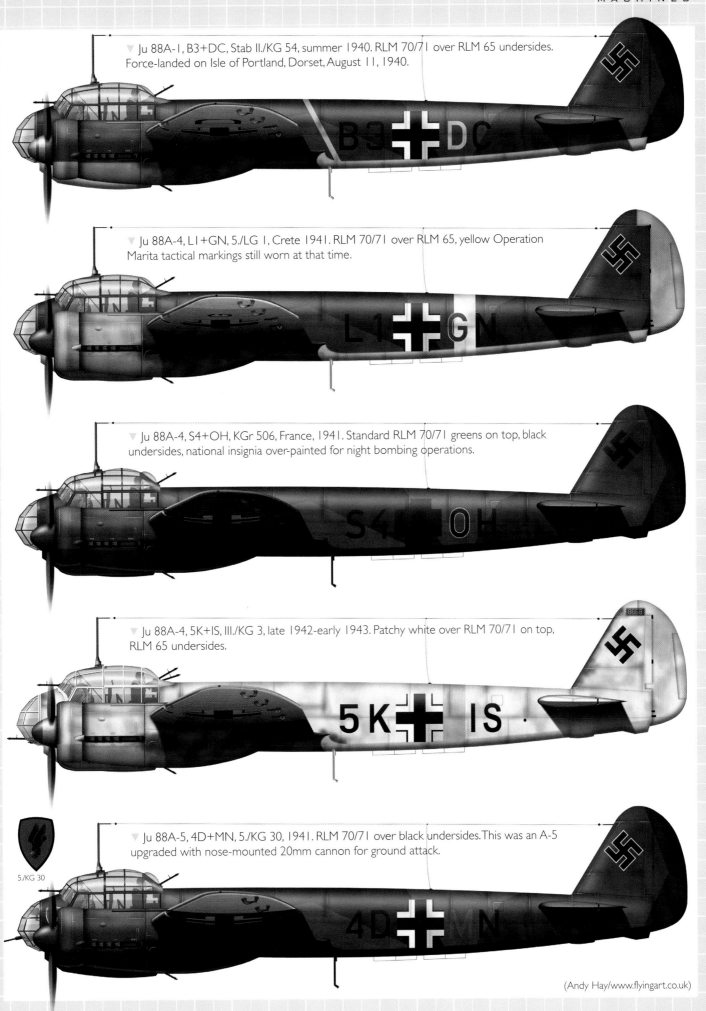

▼ Ju 88A-1, B3+DC, Stab II./KG 54, summer 1940. RLM 70/71 over RLM 65 undersides.
Force-landed on Isle of Portland, Dorset, August 11, 1940.

▼ Ju 88A-4, L1+GN, 5./LG 1, Crete 1941. RLM 70/71 over RLM 65, yellow Operation
Marita tactical markings still worn at that time.

▼ Ju 88A-4, S4+OH, KGr 506, France, 1941. Standard RLM 70/71 greens on top, black
undersides, national insignia over-painted for night bombing operations.

▼ Ju 88A-4, 5K+IS, III./KG 3, late 1942-early 1943. Patchy white over RLM 70/71 on top,
RLM 65 undersides.

▼ Ju 88A-5, 4D+MN, 5./KG 30, 1941. RLM 70/71 over black undersides. This was an A-5
upgraded with nose-mounted 20mm cannon for ground attack.

5./KG 30

(Andy Hay/www.flyingart.co.uk)

WEVER'S VISION

The Ju 88 was one of the most important tactical bombers of the World War Two era, but its beginnings went back to the mid-1930s

On June 3, 1936 an air crash took place that was to have far-reaching consequences for years to come.

On that day a Heinkel He 70 single-engined transport aircraft fell to earth near Dresden in eastern Germany, killing a top Luftwaffe official. He was Generalleutnant Walther Wever, the head of Nazi Germany's air staff. An enthusiastic supporter of a strategic air force able to take the offensive to the enemy into its own 'back yard', Wever had been a strong opponent of high-ranking Nazi officials such as the influential Ernst Udet. The latter favoured a tactical air force for close support, which would be devoid of long-range heavy bombers to strike at the enemy's industries. Wever's death resulted in a dramatic and far-reaching change of emphasis in Nazi Germany's war-making strategy, resulting in the Luftwaffe forever after being a tactical-orientated organisation…without a strategic arm of powerful and numerous

long-range heavy bombers.

As far as the Luftwaffe's tactical bombing capacity was concerned, following Wever's death several designs of light/medium bombers for support and non-strategic operations gained vital prominence. One of these was Junkers'

streamlined, very modern-looking tactical bomber, the Ju 88.

Expansion plans

The origins of this successful warplane date to the massive expansion of Germany's armed forces, following the accession to power of Adolf Hitler and the Nazis during early 1933. One of the branches of service expanded continuously from thence onwards was the Luftwaffe, at first clandestinely and then, from 1935, openly. The branch of government responsible for overseeing the Luftwaffe and its operational requirements was the Nazis' air ministry, the Reichsluftfahrtministerium (RLM). Although this organisation all too easily became embroiled in debates over the merits of strategic versus tactical aviation, with emphasis on offensive or defensive capabilities, it did at least have officials willing to embrace new and advanced design and technology. A direct result of this was the 1935 requirement from the RLM's Technisches Amt (technical and

The very first Ju 88 was the Ju 88V1, D-AQEN. Its initial flight was during December 1936, design work having just started in earnest during January that year. (Malcolm V Lowe Collection)

The Ju 88A's main undercarriage retracted backwards into the wheel well and rotated as it did so, to lie flat inside the nacelle. It was a strong unit that underwent even more strengthening during A-series production. (John Batchelor Collection)

design department or office) for what was at the time called a 'schnellbomber' or fast bomber. The new design would be a streamlined, powerful tactical ground-attack machine able to support land forces in the tactical environment, and to launch bombing raids behind the lines, but these would not be the long-range strategic missions advocated by strategists such as Wever.

The idea of the schnellbomber developed during the 1930s and assumed a very fast bomber could simply outrun defending fighters, therefore obviating the need for defensive armament; this would in turn allow for a significant reduction in drag because there would be no need for gun turrets or under fuselage gondolas, and their heavy guns, ammunition, and crew members (gunners) would not be needed, resulting in improved performance. The concept also existed in Britain…de Havilland's Mosquito being a product of this line of design thinking.

Several companies responded to the RLM's requirement, most notably Messerschmitt and Junkers. The former's contender was the Bf 162, later called the 'Jaguar', a development of the Bf 110. A Focke-Wulf entry also existed, but this and the Messerschmitt contender did not progress into production. The clear winner was Junkers' proposal. The result was the Ju 88, which was to become

one of the most versatile aircraft of World War Two, fulfilling various different frontline roles additional to the originally intended tasking of daylight level bomber, with a performance that, at the time of its birth, surpassed that of many contemporary single-engined fighters expected to oppose it.

Design quality

Actual design work on what became the Ju 88 was undertaken from early 1936, although Junkers' designers had a basic idea of what they wanted to create during the winter of 1935-1936. The actual work was led by two talented aircraft designers, WH Evers, and Alfred Gassner. The latter, an American based in Europe at that time, was well versed in the latest advances in

metal stressed skin construction being made in the US and this, combined with the established pedigree of the Junkers company in metal working, led to an excellent state-of-the-art project.

Much of the design work for the Ju 88 took place at Dessau, but Junkers also outsourced its drawing offices, particularly later in World War Two due to the disruption of Allied bombing, and used locations such as Raguhn outside Dessau itself. The Ju 88 was built eventually in various sub-types, series manufacture being continuous from 1939 until 1945. It was therefore one of a comparatively small number of warplanes in frontline service throughout the war. As testimony to its design layout, during production the basic structure of the aircraft **》》**

The Ju 88V6 was one of the most important of the family's experimental/ development Versuchs airframes, and was the first with a production-style main undercarriage leg arrangement. (Malcolm V Lowe Collection)

The distinctive streamlined and only partly glazed nose shape, and the Do 17-style main undercarriage legs of the early Ju 88s are exemplified here by Ju 88V3 D-AREN. Numerically this was the first Ju 88 to be powered by the Jumo 211. (Junkers)

▲ The instrument panel of a Ju 88A-1. It was possible from the pilot's position to see right into the nose section, the so-called 'beetle's eye' nose shape comprising many small glazed panels. (Malcolm V Lowe Collection)

two Daimler Benz DB 600 engines. It was followed by a V-series (Versuchs = experimental/development) of trials aircraft that pioneered the Ju 88 in terms of development, powerplant, armament, and the many other aspects necessary to bring a new aircraft type into service, and to develop it further. Although the design flew well from the start, considerable time was spent on development work, resulting in the first frontline examples only entering Luftwaffe service later in 1939. As contracted, there was an initial batch of five Versuchs aircraft (V1 to V5), later increased to eight (V6 to V8), but eventually more were added and numbered up to the Ju 88V112 (although not all numbers in between were used). From the Ju 88V9 onwards the aircraft were 'Nullserie', sometimes referred to as Ju 88A-0 pre-production aircraft, although Junkers documentation from the time does not identify clearly when the A-0 pre-production batch began and ended. Informatively, the Ju 88V9 had the WNr 0001.

The earliest of the Versuchs Ju 88s featured a streamlined half-glazed nose section, and a main undercarriage arrangement similar to that of the Dornier Do 17-series, with a leg on each side of the mainwheel. Continuing

remained unchanged, but as will be related later in this book, the Ju 88 underwent a staggering number of detail changes, in addition to more obvious alterations such as increased defensive armament. As with many German warplanes of that era, the exact number of examples built is open to wide interpretation and debate, but certainly a total in excess of 15,000 is now generally regarded as being near the truth.

Early developments

In a remarkably short space of time, the first prototype/development Ju 88, the Ju 88V1, WNr 4941 registered D-AQEN, was built at Dessau and made ready for test flying. It first flew on December 21, 1936, powered by

◢ An excellent detail view of a Versuchs Ju 88. Note the four-bladed propeller unit. The annular radiator arrangement of the engine cowling gave the impression of a radial engine, but the Jumo 211 was in fact an inline powerplant. (via Peter Walter)

A distinctive feature of the Ju 88A series' cockpit area was the bank of radio equipment, carried on racks attached to the rear bulkhead. Here, FuG 10 radio equipment sits in the interior of a Ju 88A-1. (via Peter Walter)

the wings outboard of the engine nacelles, and hinged to the wing's front spar. These were pioneered on the Ju 88V6. Eventually, a sophisticated (for its day) automatic bombing system was installed in the production Ju 88s, which allowed a safe and accurate dive and bomb release.

Initial production

The manufacture of the Ju 88 as a bomber can be divided into two distinct sections. Initially there were the early production models – A-1, A-5, and A-4 (they were not produced in sequence) together with the A-3 dual-control conversion trainer. Following this were versions derived from both the A-5 and A-4, numbered from the A-6 onwards – together with related reconnaissance models.

The first production bomber version was the Ju 88A-1. This was a relatively austere initial series-produced model, and it demonstrated that one of the concepts of the schnellbomber theory had been eradicated, due to the type's modest defensive armament. Combat experience with other frontline types over Spain during the Spanish Civil War had taught that defensive armament was an absolute necessity, so the Ju 88 from the first was in reality a fast, but armed medium bomber.

The Ju 88A-1 of 1939 was powered by two Jumo 211B-series engines of 1,200 hp each take-off power, driving three-bladed VDM metal narrow-bladed variable-pitch propellers; some early V-series aircraft and A-0 'Nullserie' airframes featured four-bladed propellers. The A-1's wing span was 59ft 10½in (18.25m), and the basic armament comprised flexible- »

development led to the Ju 88V4 and V6, which first flew during February and June 1938 respectively, and these (together with the V7 and later development aircraft) pioneered the production layout for the earliest series-construction Ju 88s. In particular, the main undercarriage was changed to a more conventional single leg arrangement (introduced by the V6), which itself went through necessary strengthening early in the production of initial Ju 88A versions. Introduced onto the starboard lower fuselage was a streamlined 'gondola' ('Bola' in German parlance). This incorporated a bomb-aiming window at its front end with provision for a Lotfe bomb sight, and in its rear end, a drop-down crew entrance with its own ladder. The distinctive Ju 88 'trademark' of the so-called 'beetle's eye' nose shape of many small glazed panels was also introduced at that time, again on the V4 and V6.

There was also a major change of powerplant. The DB 600-series engines used for the first two aircraft were essentially fighter engines, needed for the production of other warplanes. Thus, with the V3, the powerful and more appropriate Jumo 211 inverted V12 liquid-cooled engine was installed. This was a Junkers unit, and many of the subsequent marks of Ju 88 were to feature this excellent power source.

Change of emphasis

The dramatic number of mainly small but significant detail changes to the original design slowed development

work and prototype flying for the Ju 88 programme. However, although many changes were simply detail modifications, a significant alteration came with the demand from the RLM that the Ju 88 should be modified to perform not just level daylight bombing, but also dive bombing. This major change may well have been inspired by Ernst Udet himself, who rose in the RLM's ranks following the death of Wever, to become the head of the RLM's Technisches Amt. Udet was a true dive-bombing enthusiast, and champion of the Junkers Ju 87 Stuka, whose main function was to perform this dangerous mission profile which, of necessity, places considerable strain on airframe and crew members alike.

Such a significant change resulted in much head-scratching and re-design at Junkers. A very visible result was the fitting of prominent dive brakes under

With the reconfiguring of the Ju 88A into a dive bomber, it was necessary to fit retractable dive brakes beneath each wing, just outboard of the engine nacelles. (John Batchelor Collection)

The forward fuselage and cockpit of a Ju 88A-1 from Kampfgeschwader 30 (KG 30). Its forward-facing MG 15 of the A-Stand windscreen location can be seen, plus two similar weapons at the rear of the cockpit glazing (B-Stand)...
this being a late A-1 fitting also applicable to the early A-5.
(Malcolm V Lowe Collection)

mounted machine guns. These were an MG 15 7.92mm in the A-Stand position in the windshield; the same in the rear of the cockpit glazing pointing aft (B-Stand); and a similar weapon in the crew entrance drop-down gondola hatch (C-Stand). Production Ju 88As had a forward and a rear bomb bay, which could carry a wide variety of store sizes, or extra fuel to augment the main fuselage fuel tanks. External fuel tanks could also be mounted on four external underwing bomb carriers/pylons inboard of the engine nacelles. For the A-1, a bomb load of four 250kg or two 500kg bombs could be carried on the four external pylons. Some A-1 examples were fitted with Walter rocket packs under their wings for help with take-off when loaded (these are sometimes called Ju 88A-2). Detail changes such as an alteration to the gun mount of the C-Stand were incorporated during production.

Increased size

The Ju 88A-1 was intended to be followed by the much-improved and more powerful A-4, followed by the A-5, but because the intended Jumo 211J powerplant of the A-4 was not ready for full service entry, the A-5 followed the A-1 as an interim until the A-4 was ready. The A-5 of 1940 introduced an extended wingspan intended for the A-4, of 65ft 10½in (20.08m), with redesigned metal-covered ailerons (those of the A-1 were fabric-covered). Many detail changes appeared within the A-5 production run, such as improved radio and IFF, redesigned aerials, and slight alterations to the defensive armament mounts. The

The drop-down crew entrance, with its own ladder at the rear end of the lower fuselage gondola, featured an armament location (the C-Stand) which, on the Ju 88A-4 (or possibly later mark) shown here, included an MG 81Z twin (Zwilling) machine gun installation.
(Malcolm V Lowe Collection)

A-5 was powered initially by the Jumo 211B-series, but later examples had the Jumo 211G or H-series engines of similar rating to the B-series, but with greater output at certain heights.

The A-5 proved to be sturdier in combat than the A-1, although throughout production of the Ju 88 series its crews certainly favoured the fast and manoeuvrable Junkers twin. However, the best early production Ju 88 was the A-4 of late 1940, with its Jumo 211J engines rated at 1,401hp for take-off. This excellent level and

dive bomber was the basis of many subsequent marks, and was arguably by far the best of its kind in Germany during the mid-war period. Although some early examples were powered by the Jumo 211F engine, the Jumo 211J gave this mark more power, speed and load-carrying capacity. This engine had a pressurised coolant system, its induction air cooler being located beneath the engine – giving the A-4 a deeper engine cowling shape with a prominent fairing over the air cooler equipment and pipe-work. Most A-4s also had wide-chord wooden VS 11 propellers.

There were many detail changes compared to the A-5, and further alterations during the A-4 production run included a slightly revised rudder balance shape. Increased armour protection was provided for the crew, later examples actually featuring a specially armoured seat for the pilot. A maximum bomb load (internal and external) could reach 7,936lb (3,600kg) for short-range missions, although many combinations of weapons and fuel tankage were possible both in the bomb bays and carried externally. The A-4 was also better armed defensively; its rear part of the cockpit featured a new bulged shape to allow two

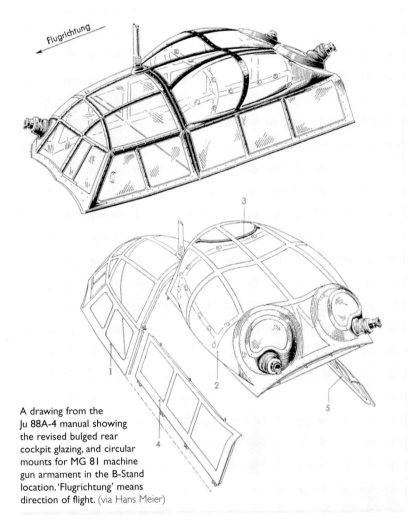

A drawing from the Ju 88A-4 manual showing the revised bulged rear cockpit glazing, and circular mounts for MG 81 machine gun armament in the B-Stand location. 'Flugrichtung' means direction of flight. (via Hans Meier)

powerful MG 81 7.92mm machine guns to be mounted in special circular mounts in the B-Stand position. One of these weapons could also be fitted in the A-Stand windscreen location, and a twin MG 81Z was available on a revised mount for the gondola C-Stand position. Additionally, a variety of other weapons (such as the MG 131 13mm machine gun), and revised weapons locations were adopted, sometimes on an individual or unit-level basis, to allow for greater defensive possibilities for the four-man crew.

It was the Ju 88A-1 and A-5 that bore the brunt of the early combat life of the Ju 88, including the Battle of Britain, while as explained later in this book, the Ju 88A-4 was a major asset in the war against the Soviet Union.

An armourer works on the underwing bomb racks of a Ju 88A-series aircraft. These stores pylons could carry bombs, mines or could be plumbed for the carriage of range-increasing external fuel tanks. (Malcolm V Lowe Collection)

The Ju 88A-1 and A-5 had smooth lower engine cowlings, as seen here on a KG 51 'Edelweiß' example. An additional gun mount can be seen on the rear side of the cockpit glazing, one of several possible locations used for additional defensive machine guns. (Malcolm V Lowe Collection)

INTO THE FRAY

The Ju 88 was arguably the best of the Luftwaffe's main bomber types of World War Two, and served in major campaigns during the early years

The annular radiator installation of the Ju 88A series is well illustrated by this A-5, probably of KG 30. This circular cowling frontage gave the impression of a radial engine layout, but the power plant was the inline Jumo 211-series engine. (Malcolm V Lowe Collection)

Junkers' Ju 88 was destined to fly and fight on all the war fronts that preoccupied the Luftwaffe during World War Two.

During the early months of the war, Nazi Germany's Luftwaffe included three major twin-engined bomber types in frontline service. These were the Dornier Do 17 and the Junkers Ju 88, both classed as 'schnellbomber', and the slower but nonetheless capable Heinkel He 111. All three were in the vanguard of the early, victorious campaigns during the war's opening stages,

Service entry

Successful if protracted initial assessment of the Ju 88 design took place with the various Versuchs prototype/development aircraft, and the pre-series Ju 88A-0 'Nullserie' machines. This included company testing, and thence to government evaluation by official trials establishments, such as the E-stelle at Rechlin. The Ju 88 was eventually cleared for Luftwaffe integration and the writing of working manuals during summer 1939. Severe delays with the development of the type,

not least due to the addition of dive bombing to its original level-flight attack capability, resulted in just a small number of Ju 88As reaching Luftwaffe service when World War Two began during September 1939.

The initial Luftwaffe trials and evaluation unit for the Ju 88 was Erprobungskommando (EKdo) 88 at Greifswald. On the outbreak of war, 12 early Ju 88As and crews from EKdo 88 were rapidly upgraded to combat status as a staffel within the administrative district of Luftflotte 2, initially under the designation 1./KG

25 and deployed to Jever. Together with a second staffel created from EKdo 88, this formed the nucleus of the first gruppe within a brand-new bomber wing, Kampfgeschwader 30. It was to be this unit that took the Ju 88A to war, and it became one of the type's chief exponents in the coming years.

KG 30 was initially tasked with hunting Royal Navy ships in the North Sea, a maritime strike role which was to be a feature of Ju 88 operations for much of the rest of the war, alongside the more widely publicised operations over land. Based at Westerland on the island of Sylt, KG 30 flew the Ju 88's first wartime sorties, including a famous attack on the aircraft carrier HMS *Ark Royal* on September 26, which was subsequently claimed in

Relatively intact shot-down Ju 88A examples were of great intelligence interest to the British during 1940. This A-1 of KG 51 was one of the first to be examined in detail having belly-landed; note its starboard engine has already been removed for analysis. (John Batchelor Collection)

error by Nazi propaganda to have been sunk. What was probably the first combat loss of a Ju 88 took place on October 9 when a Ju 88A-1 from 3./KG 30 was brought down into the sea by anti-aircraft fire from Royal Navy ships. The first Luftwaffe aircraft to crash on British soil was a Ju 88A-1 believed to be from 2./KG 30, which was shot down by anti-aircraft fire over the island of Hoy on October 17.

These early exchanges were just the start of the Ju 88's extensive wartime Luftwaffe career. Although skirmishes over the North Sea continued into 1940, very different major operations commenced during April 1940. On

April 9 began Operation Weserübung, Germany's attack on Denmark and Norway, which opened the Norwegian campaign. The Ju 88As of KG 30 were fully involved in these operations, especially in providing anti-shipping strike capability against Royal Navy warships, which were part of Britain's response to this major assault. They were joined later in April by Ju 88A-1s from a portion of the second major unit to transition to the type, namely Lehrgeschwader 1 (LG 1). Nominally a trials and training outfit, LG 1 became a highly successful frontline bomber wing in its own right, and its 3rd Gruppe took its

newly assigned Ju 88A-1s into battle later in the Norwegian campaign. Indeed, Ju 88s were involved in the Norwegian fighting right up to the end of operations, II./KG 30 supporting German land forces during the bitter fighting for Narvik, which ended in German victory in Norway. By then the Ju 88A had played an important part in this overall German success. Nevertheless, the total cost had been comparatively heavy, and even late in the campaign, on May 16, losses were still suffered when Fleet Air Arm Blackburn Skua fighters from HMS *Ark Royal*'s 803 Naval Air Squadron shot down two KG 30 Ju 88As. ⏩

A Ju 88A-1 of 1./KG 30, which had evidently made a belly-landing with both motors still working, hence the bent propellers. This genuine contemporary colour image shows well the dark upper surface splinter pattern of two green shades. (John Batchelor Collection)

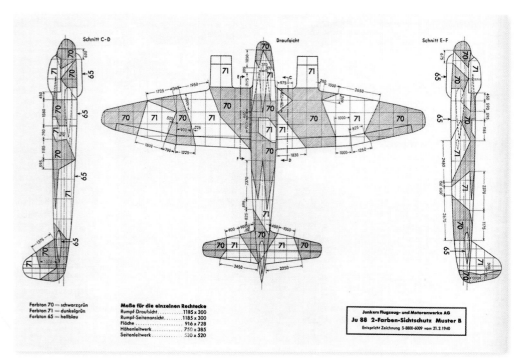

Schnitt C-D

Draufsicht

Schnitt E-F

Farbton 70 = schwarzgrün
Farbton 71 = dunkelgrün
Farbton 65 = hellblau

Maße für die einzelnen Rechtecke
Rumpf-Draufsicht..........1185 x 300
Rumpf-Seitenansicht.......1185 x 300
Fläche....................916 x 728
Höhenleitwerk.............750 x 385
Seitenleitwerk............530 x 520

Junkers Flugzeug- und Motorenwerke AG
Ju 88 2-Farben-Sichtschutz Muster B
Entspricht Zeichnung S-8800-6009 vom 21.2.1940

Blitzkrieg

Apart from II./KG 30, all other Ju 88 units were withdrawn from the Norwegian fighting, prior to the final action in Norway for the coming campaigns in the West. On May 10, 1940, Germany launched its Blitzkrieg assault against the Low Countries and France, and from thence onwards the Ju 88 was to be involved heavily in the fighting. The Luftwaffe's order of battle for these operations included the established KG 30 and LG 1 within the north Germany-based Luftflotte 2, and the third Gruppe of KG 4, which was just in the process of conversion from the He 111. Further south, within Luftflotte 3, the famous bomber wing KG 51 'Edelweiß' was just converting to Ju 88A-1s, as more of these early production aircraft became available for action.

KG 30 with its Ju 88A-1s in particular was in the thick of the fighting from the first moments, advanced elements of II./KG 30 taking off from their Oldenburg base at 0431 hours on May 10 to attack anti-aircraft defences on airfields around Rotterdam and Delft. The brief but spirited Dutch defence resulted in several Ju 88s being shot down on this first day, 9./KG 4 especially suffering four losses, including three to Dutch fighter aircraft. Targets in Belgium were also hit, while further south KG 51 Ju 88A-1s flying from bases in central and southern Germany supported the German armoured thrusts into the Ardennes,

A Junkers drawing from early 1940 showing the 'Muster B' splinter camouflage pattern for the Ju 88A-1, which remained relevant during subsequent manufacture. The shades were two greens on top, RLM 70 Schwarzgrün and 71 Dunkelgrün, and RLM 65 Hellblau light blue underneath.
(via John Batchelor)

and thence deep into France during the following days and weeks.

As German troops made ground rapidly, supporting bomber units were also able to move forward to advanced bases. It must be stressed, however, that at this stage the Ju 88 was still in the minority, both the Do 17 and the He 111 bombers being far more numerous. On May 10, for example, just 133 Ju 88As were effective out of a total Luftwaffe bomber force of 1,097 available aircraft.

It was during the Battle of France that Ju 88s first encountered RAF fighters in quantity, very often Hawker Hurricanes, as well as French fighters, and at that point losses in aerial combat burgeoned. This led to the

increases in defensive firepower added to the Ju 88s, sometimes at unit level (as described in the previous chapter). Accurate French anti-aircraft fire also accounted for various losses. Nonetheless, the first phase of the German invasion went very successfully, and several Ju 88 units were diverted necessarily from their strikes on airfields and bridges, to join in the German attacks on the Dunkirk evacuation (Operation Dynamo) in late May/early June. Following this they ranged increasingly westwards, with missions against airfields, bridgeheads, and even more so against infrastructure such as aircraft factories, which fell within range as the Blitzkrieg rolled forward inexorably. Strikes were made on June 3 against targets at Le Bourget, just outside Paris, and following the ending of fighting in Norway, II./KG 30 was able to join the air war over France. In mid-June this unit bombed the port and harbour facilities at the western maritime city of Cherbourg.

Sadly, a tragic incident followed when, on June 17, Ju 88A-1s from KG 30 attacked the port of Saint-Nazaire, where hasty evacuations of Allied personnel and French civilians were underway. Precision dive-bombing by Ju 88s resulted in the sinking of the former liner RMS/HMT *Lancastria* and with considerable loss of life, especially women and children; an incident mired in controversy and covered in secrecy to this day. The successful ending of the Battle of France for the Germans, led to Luftwaffe assets moving into French

This Ju 88A-5 of 7./KG 4 was shot down by anti-aircraft fire during a raid against RAF installations in Yorkshire, on October 27, 1940. By then the Ju 88 force was operating increasingly on evening and night-time raids, hence the bat and crescent moon unit insignia.
(John Batchelor Collection)

and Belgian airfields for coming attacks on the British Isles.

Operations over Britain

By the time of the Battle of Britain, which lasted from July to October 1940, the Ju 88A was becoming more prominent numerically. Production increasingly provided attrition replacements for aircraft lost up to that time, and during the latter part of the battle, the improved Ju 88A-5 started to gain notoriety. At the height of air operations, on August 13 ('Adler Tag' – Eagle Day), the Luftwaffe recorded 252 Ju 88As as being serviceable, but this was still well down on the 434 He 111s available. At that time KG 77 was transitioning from the Do 17 to the Ju 88 within Luftflotte 2, while elements of KG 4 and KG 76 also had Ju 88As on strength within Luftflotte 2, operating from recently captured French airfields. In Luftflotte 3, KG 51's Ju 88As were also based in France together with KG 54 'Totenkopf', a new '88A operator, and the then French-based LG 1. However, KG 30's Ju 88As were stationed at Aalborg in Denmark under Luftflotte 5, for operations against locations further north in the British Isles.

Specific targets included airfields in southern England, but aircraft factories and other important infrastructure such as radar stations were also hit. All were within range for the Ju 88s from the newly secured French airfields, but the air war over Britain was very different to that of the preceding months. British defences were more robust, radar warned successfully of incoming raids, operations had to be staged with a long over-water flight before targets could be reached and, most tellingly, the RAF fielded the superb Supermarine Spitfire and Hawker Hurricane. RAF pilots took the air war to the Luftwaffe bombers in a way not seen before, and the number of Ju 88As that crashed in British fields began to grow. Indeed, overall the British defences took a steady toll of the Junkers bombers. KG 54's first major day on operations with the Ju 88A, for example, was August 11, when several targets in Dorset were attacked; the unit lost five aircraft to the increasingly successful air and ground defences. Official figures are conflicting, but Luftwaffe records suggest as many as 303 examples were lost between July and ⏩

The Ju 88's shape and layout lent itself to relatively safe belly-landings, although the aircraft would nevertheless experience serious damage. This KG 51 Ju 88A-5 with blacked-out fuselage markings has suffered in this way. (via Peter Walter)

An early production Ju 88A-1 displays its underwing external bomb carriers inboard of the engines, and offset gondola containing (at its forward end) the oval bomb-aiming window and bomb-sight installation. (Malcolm V Lowe Collection)

October 1940, although some may have been in flying accidents.

By the end of October, the failure of the Luftwaffe to defeat the RAF heralded the conclusion of the Battle of Britain and the ending of the immediate threat of invasion. Raids were already being switched to London, and the need to operate at night had been demonstrated.

Night Blitz

The increasing diversion for the Ju 88A units to night operations

Blitz against Britain that the German kampfgeschwader started to receive the most potent of the early Ju 88 bomber versions, the A-4. This gave greater operational flexibility with the type's overall higher performance, due to its Jumo 211J engines and better defensive armament.

Effective counter

As British defences increased in effectiveness, so German losses at night began to escalate. On the British side, anti-aircraft guns working in

conjunction with searchlights became more numerous and proficient. The main achievement of Britain's night-time defences, though, lay with the successful development of radar equipment small and light enough to be carried in a viable war machine. That effective aircraft was the Bristol Beaufighter. As this powerful and potentially lethal twin-engined fighter came into service, so the night skies over Britain became increasingly dangerous for Luftwaffe bomber crews. The first Ju 88A to fall to a Beaufighter did so on November 19. Nevertheless, on the night of April 16-17, 1941, London suffered its heaviest nocturnal Blitz raid. Five Ju 88s were lost…two to Beaufighter night fighters, three of the losses being from KG 77.

This phase of the Ju 88's war came to a dramatic end during 1941, for most of the units involved, due to the major shift of Luftwaffe assets from the West to fight in campaigns in the East, as explained later in this book. ◖▬

Three KG 51 Ju 88As fly in formation, two with blacked-out markings typical of nocturnal Blitz operations. These aircraft would have been carrying high explosive and incendiary bombs. (Malcolm V Lowe Collection)

A Ju 88A-1 shows off its lines, including the short wing of the A-1 version, and its '9K' fuselage code for KG 51. It actually belonged to 8./ KG 51, and its WNr on the top of the fin was 299. (via Peter Walter)

heralded a new and deadly phase of the air war. This took place during the final weeks of 1940 and continued well into 1941…and then sporadically until mid-1944. With little or no aids to pinpoint targets in darkness, the emphasis was very much on the bombing of towns and cities, which presented larger and much easier targets. Some raids on which Ju 88s flew subsequently have become infamous. Among these was the devastating November 14 attack on Coventry.

It was during the time of the night

Available for use with the Ju 88A-5, but rarely employed, was the ability to carry a bomb outboard of the engine cowling, exemplified by this rare view of an unidentified aircraft taxiing to the runway for take-off on a night raid during the Blitz. (Malcolm V Lowe Collection)

THE MEN BEHIND THE METAL

Ernst Zindel (left) in conversation with a colleague. Zindel's name is often associated with the actual design of the Ju 88, but a team of designers was responsible for this warplane's creation. (Malcolm V Lowe Collection)

Hugo Junkers was one of aviation's great pioneers, but despite his standing he was ousted unceremoniously as head of his own company by the Nazis. He is seen here in earlier life. (John Batchelor Collection)

The rise of the Nazis ensured an ignominious demise for Junkers' founder, but promotion for another notable company employee

The unhappy events that consumed the Junkers company during the early days of the Third Reich were a personal tragedy for Hugo Junkers himself.

Rightly regarded as an influential pioneer, this high status held no interest for the Nazis, who ungenerously wanted his company and patents for themselves…at any cost.

Junkers was born in February 1859 and his interest in aviation blossomed in the early years of the 20th century. He appears to have initially explored the idea of all-metal aircraft as early as 1908, placing him at the forefront of aeronautical development. Always innovative, he registered many patents – which would prove to be a part of his undoing years later. Under his supervision during World War One, his company pioneered the development of all-metal warplanes, and continued

this work in the post-war years, putting Junkers years ahead of many rivals. The Nazis were eager to seize his business (and his many patents) following their accession to power during early 1933. Unsurprisingly, Junkers resisted this attack on his assets and was eventually placed under house arrest. He was finally forced

to hand over not just his company, but his valuable patents as well. He died during February 1935.

Within the Junkers company, one of the most influential characters in the creation of the Ju 88 was Dipl-Ing Ernst Zindel. Holding senior posts at the organisation following Hugo Junkers' departure (although he had worked with Junkers beforehand), Zindel was a significant and high-ranking member of the technical team at Dessau, which included designers, construction planners and those responsible for overseeing day-to-day production. This included work on the Ju 88 and on that other significant Junkers warplane, the Ju 87 Stuka. He was responsible to the overall chief Dr Heinrich Koppenberg, who was chairman of Junkers' supervisory board, appointed after the Nazi take-over.

In this respect Zindel theoretically became an overseer of aircraft design alongside Heinrich Hertel, and as such he has often been called somewhat erroneously the Ju 88's designer; in reality, it was the design team that actually worked on the general creation of the type. Zindel was essentially the chief of Junkers' construction programmes, and was very 'hands on' with daily production schedules, as the 'figurehead' of production – to the extent of sometimes appearing in Junkers' 'shop floor' photographs. ◼

Ernst Zindel appears to have been 'hands on' with the production of the Ju 88. He is seen here examining a Ju 88A while standing on the crew entrance ladder. (Malcolm V Lowe Collection)

ZERSTÖRER UND NACHTJÄGER

Following its initial successes as a light/medium bomber, the Ju 88 grew into several new roles including that of a heavy fighter and nocturnal hunter

With a sound basic layout, Junkers was able to expand the Ju 88's operational profile.

Eventually a whole family of different versions was developed, making the type one of the most versatile combat aircraft of World War Two. Only Britain's superlative de Havilland Mosquito was able to grow similarly (and successfully) into several distinct roles, some of which were not necessarily envisaged when the original design came into being.

Although the Ju 88 began life under the 'schnellbomber' concept, one of the combat profiles that Junkers' designers identified early during the type's development was its potential use as a well-armed heavy fighter. This general concept, encompassing a twin-engined type as a 'zerstörer' (destroyer) was of great importance in the thinking of the RLM, as evidenced by the development of the Messerschmitt Bf 110. Although larger and heavier then the established Bf 110, the Ju 88 offered considerable advantages in weapon-carrying and performance.

Junkers' designers began work on a zerstörer derivative of the basic Ju 88 layout comparatively early in the type's evolution. This involved practical modification work on one of the early Versuchs prototype/development aircraft, the Ju 88V7. This aircraft had quite a chequered career, acting as a development asset for several programmes and, at one time, was converted into a special transport aircraft. Further work was carried out with other prototype/development airframes, notably the Ju 88V58.

Various possible weapons concepts were examined, initially with guns protruding through the beetle's eye nose glazing common to Ju 88A-series bombers, but wisely this was soon replaced by a 'solid' and neatly rounded sheet metal nose. With a combination of guns and cannon armament offset slightly to starboard in the completely revised nose shape, the new design promised heavy firepower coupled with easy aiming. The pilot was provided with a fighter-style Revi gun sight for aligning this formidable battery of weapons on

New-build Ju 88C-6 heavy fighters/ zerstörers, showing the Jumo 211J engine installation and VS 11 propeller blades, which were also characteristic of the A-4 this version was related to, as well as the gondola shape of the C-6. (all Malcolm V Lowe Collection unless stated)

guns in separate installations (as on some A-4 bombers). The redesigned gondola beneath the forward fuselage included a C-Stand location for a choice of rear-facing, flexible-mounted machine guns in the entry hatch (the choice of such weaponry for the Ju 88C being virtually as wide as that for the Ju 88A bombers). Forward-firing fixed 20mm MG FF cannons were sometimes attached in the front of the gondola, there being no need for a bomb-aiming position – although the fuselage bomb bay did still exist and was available for use, as were underwing stores/weapons carriers inboard of the engines. The initial C-6 was simply a heavy fighter and zerstörer, but several earlier C-series aircraft had proved useful as makeshift night fighters, albeit without radar; the C-6 duly took this one stage further with the introduction of airborne radar.

Night fighter

The Ju 88C-6 was therefore the first major version of the Ju 88 family to carry on-board radar for night fighting. Known to the British and Americans as AI (Air Intercept) equipment, this apparatus was developed considerably in Germany as well as by the Allies. The mid- to late-war years produced a veritable battle of 'black boxes' as each side attempted to gain the upper hand in electronic equipment which, from the German perspective, allowed fighters to operate at night in opposition to nocturnal raids by RAF heavy bombers. Ultimately, several types of radar were employed on the C-6, and there were different equipment fits and alterations in armament, which often left ⟫

The Ju 88V19 was employed as a development aircraft for the Ju 88C heavy fighter/zerstörer programme, for which it was re-named the Z19. It is seen here with an additional (experimental) MG 151/20 cannon in the gondola…which was not used in this way on operational examples.

potential air and ground targets.

The new series was given the title Ju 88C. Important in the development phase was the Ju 88Z19 ('Z' standing for Zerstörer) prototype/development machine. The initial model was the C-1 heavy fighter, 20 of which (in some sources) are stated to have been converted from Ju 88A-1 bombers, retaining their Jumo 211 engines. Similarly, 20 Ju 88A airframes, possibly of A-5 origin with their greater wingspan compared to the A-1 (although this is disputed by some official records), were converted to form the C-2. This sub-type standardised the nose weapons as one 20mm MG FF cannon and three 7.92mm MG 17 machine guns. The C-3 was a proposed version with BMW 801 engines but was not built, while the C-4 was the first C-series model to be series manufactured, some 60 being built from scratch while the same number were converted from the A-5…and with the longer-span wings of the latter. The C-5 was important in introducing the BMW 801 radial engine into the C-series, which was to have a significant continuation in later Ju 88 night fighter development, but just a handful were converted, to act more as development aircraft.

By the time of the Ju 88C-6's development, it was becoming clear to the Luftwaffe the heavy fighter was an important warplane. Higher priority

was afforded to the type, and the C-6 grew into a significant programme that eventually included day fighter/ zerstörer and intruder operations, and night fighting.

The C-6 owed much of its effectiveness to being based on the Ju 88A-4 bomber, which was itself a great improvement over the preceding bomber Ju 88 versions. The C-6 was similarly powered by the Jumo 211J inline engine, either the 211J-1 or J-2 being available, with wide-chord wooden VS 11 propeller blades as also fitted to the Ju 88A-4. The forward-firing armament remained similar to that established originally for the Ju 88C-series, but a revised B-Stand position in the rear of the cockpit mounted two 7.92mm MG 81 machine

Just a small number of Ju 88C-5 night fighters were completed, these featuring a clean lower forward fuselage without the usual gondola, but able to accommodate a small weapons pack containing two machine guns, possibly of the 7.92mm MG 17 variety.

The Ju 88V58 WNr 700001, factory coded GI+BW, was central to Ju 88G development. It had the tail shape of the Ju 188, and was fitted with an unusual arrangement of radar antenna 'antlers' on its nose.

This Ju 88C-4 wore the night fighter arm's insignia below its cockpit, and was assigned to III./NJG 2. It had an armoured windscreen typical of night fighters, plus modified rear canopy glazing, for two machine guns to be mounted rather than the one intended originally for the B-Stand position.

Ju 88 Unit Codes

Code	Unit (with examples of marks flown)
A3+	KG 200 (A-4/G-6/S-3)
A6+	Aufklärungsgruppe 120 (D-1)
B3+	KG 54 (A-4/A-14)
C9+	NJG 5 (G-1/G-6)
D5+	NJG 3 (G-6)
F1+	KG 76 (A-1/A-4/A-5)
F2+	Ergänzungs-Fernaufklärungsgruppe (D-1/T-1)
F6+	Aufklärungsgruppe 122 (A-5/D-1)
F8+	KG 40 (C-6/R-2/G-1)
G2+	Aufklärungsgruppe 124 (D-1)
G9+	NJG 1 (A-4/C-6/R-1/G-1/G-6)
K9+	3./Aufklärungsgruppe ObdL (Kdo Rowehl) (B/D-1)
L1+	LG 1 (A-1/A-4/A-5)
M2+	KGr 106 (A-4)
M7+	KGr 806 (A-4)
R4+	NJG 2 (C-1/C-2/C-4/C-6/R-2/G-1/G-6)
S4+	KGr 506 (A-5/A-4/D-1)
T1+	Aufklärungsgruppe 10 (D-1)
T5+	1. and 2./Aufklärungsgruppe ObdL (A-4/B/C-7/D-1/T-1)
T5+	1./Fernaufklärungsgruppe 100 (D-1/D-5)
T9+	Versuchsverband ObdL/OKL
U5+	KG 2 (A-4/G-6)
V4+	KG 1 (A-5/A-4)
W7+	NJG 100 (G-1/G-6)
Z6+	KG 66 (A-4/S-3)
1B+	Wekusta 5 (A-4/D-1)
1H+	KG 26 (A-4/A-14)
2J+	ZG 1 (C-6)
2N+	ZG 76 (C-6/R-2/G-1)
2Z+	NJG 6 (C-6/G-1/G-6)
3C+	NJG 4 (C-6/R-2/G-1/G-6)
3E+	KG 6 (A-4/A-14/S-0/S-1/S-3)
3U+	II./ZG 26 (C-6)
3Z+	KG 77 (A-1/A-5/A-4/A-17/S-1)
4D+	KG 30 (A-5/A-4)
4N+	Aufklärungsgruppe 22 (D-1)
4R+	NJG 2 (C-6/G-1/G-6)
4T+	Wekusta 51 (D-1)
4U+	Aufklärungsgruppe 123 (A-1/D-1/D-2/H-1/T-1)
5F+	Aufklärungsgruppe 14 (D-1/D-3)
5J+	KG 4 (A-4)
5K+	KG 3 (A-1/A-5/A-4)
5M+	Wekusta 26 (A-4/D-1)
6N+	KG 100 (A-4)
7A+	1./Aufklärungsgruppe 121 (A-1/A-5/D-1)
7J+	NJG 102 (G-1/G-6)
7T+	KGr 606 (A-4)
8H+	Aufklärungsgruppe 33 (D-1/S-3)
9K+	KG 51 (A-1/A-5/A-4)
9W+	NJG 101 (G-1/G-6)

Note: The examples of marks flown are as exact as possible, and not intended as an exhaustive list of every aircraft flown by each unit.

groundcrew bemused in finding that no two aircraft in an operational unit were the same. Initially the FuG 202 Lichtenstein BC was fitted, then the FuG 212 Lichtenstein C-1, followed by the FuG 220 Lichtenstein SN-2. Accompanying these were the associated antennae arrays attached to the aircraft's nose, although these 'Hirschgeweihe' (stag's antlers) as they were known created considerable drag. Some aircraft received tail-mounted radar-warning receivers, while others displayed altered aerials for Identification Friend or Foe and other equipment. Occasionally, the sub-type names Ju 88C-6b and C-6c are used in published sources for these radar-equipped models, with the radar-less original heavy fighter and zerstörer named C-6a.

BMW power

The undoubted success of the Ju 88C as a makeshift (but very successful) radar-equipped night fighter led to a related version, the Ju 88R, which was a BMW 801-powered machine rather than having the Jumo 211 of the C series. This additional version existed alongside the Ju 88C series, and indeed, some early Ju 88R airframes appear to have been converted from existing Ju 88Cs. In effect the Ju 88R was a night fighter equivalent of the developed Ju 88S bomber and Ju 88T recce platform described later in this book. The R-1 was powered by the BMW 801A radial engine of 1,600

hp for take-off, and was generally similar to Ju 88C-6 night fighters with FuG 202 Lichtenstein BC and FuG 212 Lichtenstein C-1. The type entered service in the first half of 1943; the R-2 was powered by the BMW 801D radial engine and was similar to C-6 night fighters sporting FuG 220 Lichtenstein SN-2 later on. With this power it could reach a creditable 360mph (580km/h) according to figures from Junkers' own documentation. Production of these versions ceased during early 1944, in favour of the definitive night fighter Ju 88, the G series.

Musical cannons

A significant weapons innovation incorporated on several marks of Ju 88 night fighter, from the C-6 onwards, was the Schräge Musik installation of oblique upwards-firing cannons mounted in roughly the mid-fuselage position. The term Schräge Musik came from a contemporary German saying for off-tune music, literally translating as 'slanted' or 'oblique music' and therefore very applicable to this weapons installation; the term is often translated in non-German speaking countries as 'Jazz Music'. Luftwaffe night fighters used this armament to approach and attack Allied bombers from below at night, outside the bomber crew's field of view. Most Allied bomber types encountered by Luftwaffe fighters during nocturnal interceptions (especially, but not exclusively the Avro Lancaster) lacked effective ventral defenses, making them easy prey from below. Several different Schräge Musik arrangements were fitted to German night fighters, usually employing either

The original 'antler' arrangement proposed for the G series was tested on the Ju 88V58, featuring the upper struts of the FuG 212 radar array angled upwards, to avoid the two nose cannons. The latter were not fitted on production aircraft and the antlers' arrangement seen here was not adopted.

one or two 20mm MG151/20 or MG FF cannons; the latter two-gun installation could be side-by-side, or in tandem. The weapons were mounted typically at an angle of between 70°-80° facing forward, some installations being field modifications. Aiming the cannons was by means of sighting equipment mounted on the upper canopy framing structure, above the pilot. The concept was also used on Bf 110 night fighters.

New layout

The importance of the Ju 88 as an interceptor for nocturnal missions was established by C-series night fighters, and it was clear to both the Luftwaffe and Junkers' designers that the Ju 88

layout had significant growth potential to be developed as an even more effective after-dark hunter. This led to the major upgrade designated as the Ju 88G series.

Hitherto the basic layout of the Ju 88 had remained largely the same throughout the type's development cycle. However, the 'G' introduced various improvements to the heavy/ night fighter configuration. Notably, the forward fuselage and crew compartment was redesigned to accommodate the intended radar equipment and its substantial black boxes, the necessary on-board power to house all new equipment, and the ability to carry major structures on the nose of the aircraft for the associated antennas. Night fighters in the Ju 88C-series had pioneered this arrangement, then the whole concept had to be taken further for the dedicated night fighter series, the Ju 88G. The lower fuselage gondola so distinctive of the A series was removed altogether, and a gun pack installed beneath the fuselage. All tail surfaces were revised and enlarged with, most noticeably, much greater area for the vertical tail to aid in directional stability (necessary due to the redesigned nose and its drag-producing aerials). This alteration to the tail was in parallel with ⏩

A Ju 88G-6 bearing the '7J' code of NJG 102 displays several important features, including the two-cannon Schräge Musik installation in the mid-upper fuselage, and the humped fairing for FuG 350 Naxos passive homing equipment on top of the cockpit.

A clear study of the Jumo 213A-1 engine layout on a Ju 88G-6 night fighter, also showing to advantage the FuG 220 Lichtenstein SN-2 radar antenna arrangement. Several developed models of the excellent SN-2 were employed by the G-6 during its service life, the angled dipoles here denoting a late mark.

developments for the Ju 188/Ju 388 described later in this book.

In the event, a number of specific Ju 88G versions and sub-types were created, which responded to major advances made in the electronic war being fought behind the scenes, by the scientists on both sides engaged in this deadly cat and mouse tussle. The often-substantial changes can be summarised in the following explanation of the various marks and sub-types of the Ju 88G-series. These became, in the later war years, the main focus of Ju 88 manufacture, while production Ju 88 bomber versions became of less importance militarily for the Germans, as home defence against Allied bombing secured primary importance.

Significant in the development process for the Ju 88G series was the Ju 88V58, which first flew in the new configuration during June 1943. A limited pre-production series of Ju 88G-0 airframes followed, the successful testing of which led to full-scale manufacture as soon as possible. By that stage in the war, nocturnal raids by the RAF were having a major effect on German economy and infrastructure, and even the Nazi hierarchy realised the need for considerably updated and improved night-time defence. To that end, 700 production aircraft were ordered even before flight testing was completed.

The first major series-manufactured version was the Ju 88G-1, and this set the standard for future G-models. The type was powerful, well-equipped with the latest AI radar and had heavy firepower; four forward-firing MG 151/20 cannons in a streamlined gun pack below the former fuselage bomb bay, and offset to port. Power was provided by two BMW 801D-series radial engines, the supply problems of these excellent powerplants having eased. For nocturnal interception purposes, the G-1 was fitted with baseline FuG 220 Lichtenstein SN-2 radar, and carried a crew of four. The Ju 88V59 acted as a development aircraft for modifications to the basic 'G' layout, and trialled the GM-1 nitrous oxide boost system for the engines and improved exhaust flame-damping. This initial Ju 88G model first entered combat late in 1943.

The Ju 88G-2 was a proposed version powered by Jumo 213 inline engines. This planned development was not series manufactured, but neither was the next sub-type, the Ju 88G-3…which would have been powered by the Daimler Benz DB 603E. The Ju 88G-4 shared the same fate, this proposed model including a day-fighter zerstörer layout. Instead, the next major production variant was the G-6.

This new four-seat model represented the pinnacle of German night fighter development at that time, and was built in several major sub-types depending on radar fit. Power came from two Jumo 213A-1 inline engines rated at 1,750 hp for take-off. Through the development and operational life of the type, several different main radar installations became available, due to the ever-changing nature of the electronic war. Fitted originally with standard FuG 220 Lichtenstein SN-2 radar, later the FuG 218 'Neptun' became available. The type of antler-like antenna installation on the nose of the aircraft

Illustrating the May 1945-standard Ju 88G-6 format, this captured example at Langensalza, WNr 623185, features Schräge Musik, FuG 220 Lichtenstein SN-2 radar, and a fitment at the base of the rudder for a tail-mounted radar warning device.

also went through a major evolution, with dipoles designed for the different frequencies of radars fitted. A standard Hirschgeweih eight-dipole aerial structure was the baseline, but other layouts were trialled and later the more aerodynamic 'Morgenstern' design was tried. In fact, the arrangement of the aerial fit on the Ju 88 night fighter family went through its own evolution, as scientists worked with Junkers' designers and specialists at Luftwaffe test establishments,

such as the E-Stelle at Rechlin, to perfect the various layouts. A small number of late-war aircraft were fitted, for example, with experimental Telefunken FuG 240 'Berlin' cavity magnetron-based radar, with a (for the time) advanced dish antenna

encased by a streamlined wooden nose fairing, which negated the drag-inducing aerials. The G-6 was armed with the battery of four forward-firing MG 151/20 cannon in the offset under fuselage fairing, with an MG 131 machine gun in the old B-Stand

position for rearwards defence. Many G-6 aircraft were armed with Schräge Musik, and could be fitted if required with a stores/weapons pylon inboard of the engine nacelles.

The Ju 88G-7 was to have been a follow-on major development project, powered by Jumo 213E engines. This type has been confused by some writers as the G-6, which is incorrect. Instead, a major air raid on Junkers' main factory complex at Dessau, during early March 1945 delayed the programme significantly, which was still in the process of development at the war's end.

The highest-numbered Ju 88G-series version that existed was the G-10, which was a long-endurance model with a lengthened fuselage, able to carry considerably more internal fuel due to the redesigned and extended layout. As far as can be verified, this sub-type did not enter actual service, and the various examples that existed appear to have been redirected to the unusual Mistel composite aircraft programme, which is explained later in this book. ⟫

The Ju 388 programme included among its various proposed versions a night fighter/zerstörer model, which would have been the Ju 388J. This aircraft, fitted with FuG 220 antlers on its nose, was the Ju 388V2 factory coded PE+IB. It did not enter series production. (via Peter Walter)

US personnel examine a Ju 88G-6 at Langensalza, after that Junkers facility was captured; the armoured windscreen is apparent. Just visible in the background, beneath the Ju 88's fuselage, is a USAAF P-38 Lightning.

This Mistel 2 composite has a Ju 88G-1 as its lower component, with a late Fw 190A or F as the upper piloted part of the combination. The Ju 88 has its conventional cockpit fitted rather than an explosives-filled warhead, but may have been in training rather than transit configuration.

One of the most famous of all Ju 88s was this G-1 of NJG 2, which landed in error at Woodbridge airfield, Suffolk on July 13, 1944, in a spectacular coup for Allied intelligence. Its Flensburg passive homing device was of particular interest. (John Batchelor Collection)

Operational travails

Flying by day or by night, the Ju 88 heavy/night fighters were important assets for Luftwaffe operations from 1940 onwards, again underlining the importance of the Junkers twin to Germany's war effort.

Long before the Ju 88 became a valued night fighter, the type established itself as a heavyweight daytime companion to the established Bf 110 zerstörer units.

Initial operations of note for the Ju 88C zerstörer force took place during 1940. An early exponent of the Ju 88's undoubted capability in this role was II./NJG 1, whose Ju 88C intruders ranged over Britain by night, attacking any targets they found. This unit's first operation, on July 23, 1940 resulted in the downing of two RAF Wellington bombers. Henceforward this type of intruder action proved of great value to the Germans and throughout the rest of the war, various nocturnal and twilight operations were staged, which targeted, among others, RAF and USAAF heavy bombers returning from missions.

For a time, the heavy fighter/ zerstörer force was later deployed to the Mediterranean and Southern Europe, NJG 2 operating in that theatre with its inappropriately black-painted Junkers until better sense prevailed, and the unit moved back further north.

Following the invasion of the Soviet Union by Germany on June 22, 1941, the Ju 88C was a very effective ground-attack aircraft on the Eastern Front, and could look after itself

The Ju 88C-6 heavy fighter/ zerstörer served with distinction on the Eastern Front. This C-6 of 4./KG 76, coded F1+XM, included the painting of fake bomber-style glazing on the nose, to confuse pilots of enemy fighters.

The Ju 88C was used as an intruder by NJG 2, its Junkers making flights over Britain hunting nocturnal targets. This sub-type was well suited to the role, in firepower and endurance. (John Batchelor Collection)

Visible in this view of a forced-landed Ju 88C-4, R4+MT of III./NJG 2, are the four 'holes' in the starboard nose for its forward-firing armament; the three small vents behind them being for gun gasses to escape, and the bulged rear cockpit area for increased rearwards-facing machine gun protection.

against the early generation of Soviet fighters encountered in the first two or so years of operations over the Soviet Union. Some Ju 88Cs were used in the close-support role but against a very different type of target. In little-known operations, C-series aircraft were employed for ground-attack sorties against Soviet railways, specifically shooting at troop/supply-carrying trains. In this role the battery of guns/cannon in the type's nose proved particularly useful. Several Kampfgeschwader employed Ju 88Cs for this task, and for the wider mission profile of disrupting communications. Central to this tasking was the C-6, assigned to bomber units such as KG 3, 27, 55, and 76.

In the West, V.KG 40 waged a very different war. From late 1942 onwards, its C-6 heavy fighters based at Lorient and Bordeaux-Mérignac, were used as escorts for U-boats in French coastal waters against marauding RAF Coastal Command aircraft. This mission expanded to escorting long-range Fw 200 Condor maritime patrol and anti-shipping aircraft operated by most of KG 40's other sub-units, and many encounters took place between the Junkers and RAF aircraft. The Ju 88C would more than hold its own against a Sunderland flying boat or Consolidated Liberator, and several air-to-air successes were gained by the Ju 88s. In June 1943 the unit had up to 50 C-6 airframes under its control. Eventually re-designated

as I./ZG 1, its Junkers were active in France during 1944 and involved in the German response to the D-Day landings of June 1944, before being withdrawn to Germany.

Nocturnal defence

At the start of the war, Germany did not possess a night fighter arm to defend the skies over Germany. It had not been in the strategic planning ▶▶

This Ju 88C-6 heavy fighter/zerstörer was damaged on a low-level strafing sortie but landed almost intact. The missing nose cone shows the arrangement of the forward-firing weaponry offset to starboard, and a large armour plate. Note the damaged wooden VS 11 propeller blades. (John Batchelor Collection)

Not all night fighters were fitted with radar. This Ju 88C served with NJG 2 and was a standard heavy fighter/zerstörer, painted inappropriately in overall black, even though it was parked in the Mediterranean or North African sun.

A winter-camouflaged Ju 88C-6 on the Eastern Front. Although the lower forward fuselage gondola was different on these aircraft to the Ju 88A-4 (from which they were derived), it nevertheless retained a similar crew entry access and machine gun mounting.

of the Nazi hierarchy that such a force would ever be necessary. At that time, it was in Britain alone where such a defence network was already being established, but the successful British system, using ground-based radar to detect incoming raiders, proved to be a model on which the Germans were eventually to develop a sophisticated air defence network, for day and nocturnal operations.

During the summer of 1940, a proper night defence force was created, one of its exponents being the accomplished Luftwaffe officer Wolfgang Falck. At first this nocturnal group was concerned with night intruder operations over Britain. But it wasn't until later the organisation had

to be expanded to defend the night skies over Germany, as a part of what became a major air defence network. The Germans, together with the British, became world-leaders in the development of credible 'joined up' air defence, using ground-based radar to detect incoming enemy aircraft. By day these could then be located visually by defending fighters, which were sent skywards to meet the incoming foe following ground-based radar contact. At night, sophisticated (for their time) night fighters with on-board radar equipment would use this short-range gear to detect the target, which would otherwise be invisible in the darkness, having been directed to the correct area of sky by the ground-

based radar and its controllers. In Germany, the Himmelbett night fighter control centres system was developed, and substantial terrestrial radar networks were established. Important among these was the Kammhuber Line, a defensive selection of radar installations named after Josef Kammhuber, who rose to be one of the most influential leaders of the Luftwaffe's night fighter force until his political dismissal during 1943.

The basic operating unit of the night fighter force was the Nachtjagdgeschwader (NJG), and virtually all NJG units came to operate Ju 88 night fighters. Initial Ju 88C-series night fighters were operated by various NJG including NJG 1, 3 and 6 in the West, as well as NJG 2 in the Mediterranean. With widespread introduction of the Ju 88G-series, that type became (for a time) the principal Luftwaffe night fighter, even eclipsing the long-established Bf 110.

Alongside the Ju 88 and Bf 110 twin-engined night fighters, tactics were also devised for anti-bomber operations for Luftwaffe single-engined fighters, both the Bf 109 and Fw 190. The latter used 'Wilde Sau' (Wild Boar) tactics, one of those behind this ultimately deadly mission being the celebrated pilot 'Hajo' Herrmann.

The Ju 88G entered combat during December 1943, but the G-1 did not become available in numbers until spring 1944. Nonetheless, that proved to be a very profitable time for the German night fighter force, with RAF losses of heavy bombers mounting steeply. This was ironic. During that period at night the Germans appeared to be gaining the upper hand, but otherwise the fight was being lost entirely by the Luftwaffe's day fighters. The appearance in numbers of the excellent North American P-51 Mustang, which escorted US heavy bombers all the way to their targets and back, resulted in crippling losses for the Luftwaffe's day fighters.

Ju 88 night fighters also operated on the Eastern Front. In that theatre, the elaborate homing devices used by Reich defence night fighters over Germany were not needed, the Soviet aircraft that were chased in the East having none of the radar and warning devices fitted to RAF heavy bombers that Ju 88s homed in on. Chief among these Eastern Front units was NJG 100, which nonetheless was equipped with the latest Ju 88G-6 night fighters in the latter stages of the war.

Additional equipment

As well as the aircraft's main radar for detecting and tracking targets, with a range of some 6 miles (9.6km) in some systems, Ju 88 nachtjäger were fitted with various electronic devices as tools of their trade. Among them was FuG 350 'Naxos', a passive homing device for detecting emissions from British H2S bombing radar carried in heavy bombers and pathfinder Mosquitos. This useful device came into widespread use during 1944 and persisted until the war's end. Later versions of the excellent FuG 220 Lichtenstein SN-2 radar incorporated a tail warning device, which featured an antenna positioned at the rear of the Ju 88, either at the base of the rudder or on the vertical tail. Most useful of all, until its discovery by the Allies, was FuG 227 'Flensburg', which followed emissions from 'Monica' tail warning radars carried by British bombers.

Nevertheless, for all the good this on-board equipment was supposed to achieve, there was nothing the Germans could do to prevent entire aircraft and their valuable 'black boxes' falling into Allied hands. On July 13, 1944 a Ju 88G-1 coded 4R+UR of 7./NJG 2, landed in error at RAF Woodbridge airfield in Suffolk, having become lost. Its crew of three was taken prisoner, but the aircraft and its internal equipment were of immense value. It was fitted with FuG 220 Lichtenstein SN-2 main radar, which was of great interest, but the aircraft also had Flensburg installed. This caused an immediate withdrawal of Monica equipment from all aircraft that carried it. Another useful arrival at a British airfield was a Ju 88R-1 night fighter, which was landed at RAF Dyce by its defecting pilot on May 9, 1943. This aircraft still survives and is illustrated in detail on Pages 52-54. ▶▶

A close-up view of the BMW 801 engine installation, and weapons pack, beneath the fuselage of the Ju 88V58 prototype/ development aircraft for the Ju 88G programme. On production G-series aircraft this pod contained four 20mm MG 151/20 cannon, their ammunition housed in the former bomb bay.

A Ju 88G-1 with the distinctive curved 'antlers' denoting FuG 220 Lichtenstein SN-2 radar. The crew entry hatch in the lower forward fuselage is open in this view. It has a FuG 227 Flensburg aerial on its starboard wing leading edge.
(John Batchelor Collection)

This well-known Ju 88G-1 of NJG 2 landed in error at Woodbridge airfield, Suffolk on July 13, 1944; a massive stroke of luck for the British in revealing the secrets of its on-board 'black boxes'. The three-man crew was taken prisoner. (John Batchelor Collection)

Maintenance work in progress on a Ju 88C, R4+FM, formerly of NJG 2 whose identification it wore, but actually transferred to 10./NJG 1. It had an impressive kill tally on its vertical tail, and was flown by high-scoring night fighter pilot Wilhelm Beier. (via John Batchelor)

Some Schräge Musik installations comprised just one cannon as on this Ju 88G, believed to have been operated by NJG 100. The aircraft also has a single 13mm MG 131 machine gun (fitted with a muzzle flash shroud) in the cockpit's rear defensive B-Stand gun position.

Changing fortunes

On January 1, 1945 the Luftwaffe carried out Operation Bodenplatte, the famous massive attack on forward-located Allied airfields on the Continent. This action mainly involved fighters flying as ground-attack aircraft, with bombers or night fighters acting as pathfinders. Ju 88s of various marks were involved in this largely fruitless operation, including several Ju 88Gs.

If use of the 'G' as a pathfinder for Bodenplatte had been a waste of valuable resources, so too was the use of these aircraft during daylight hours as anti-bomber fighters. By the latter part of 1944 the daylight bombing campaign of the USAAF was of immense value to the Allied war effort, but the Luftwaffe's day fighter force faced increasing numbers of US escort fighters; a situation worsened by a growing shortage of experienced pilots. So hard-pressed was the Luftwaffe in countering daytime raids by US bombers that on occasion, night fighters were drafted to bolster the day fighter force. This was a very bad idea. A lumbering Bf 110 and Ju 88 night fighter, weighed down with on-board radar and slowed by drag-inducing radar antennas, was relatively safe in the dark, but in the daytime was an easy target for marauding P-51 Mustang and P-47 Thunderbolt escort fighters. Many were shot down easily in this futile mismatch.

In the night skies, even the Ju 88G did not have everything going its own way. The threat of these aircraft to the RAF's heavy bombers and pathfinders at night did not go unnoticed, and Mosquito fighters received the tasking of hunting the hunter in the night skies over Germany. This led to a conflict within a conflict, with Ju 88G night fighters seeking out Mosquitos tasked

How many groundcrew does it take to prepare an aircraft? Judging by this image of a late-production Ju 88G-6 of NJG 100, quite a few. This unit operated on the Eastern Front, its aircraft not requiring the devices installed in Reich defence interceptors to locate British bombers.

with protecting the bombers, and the Mosquito night fighters attempting to find Ju 88s, to prevent them from shooting down RAF heavy bombers.

Operations continued virtually to the end of the war for the night fighter force, even though the war situation had turned irrevocably in favour of the Allies. One of the operational profiles that had usually been profitable for the Luftwaffe was intruder missions over the British Isles, especially those directed against heavy bombers returning from missions over Germany or Occupied Europe. A particularly successful operation was launched over the British Isles during March 1945, named Gisela. It included Ju 88G-1 and G-6 sub-types from NJG 2, 3 and 5, and resulted in around 35 Allied aircraft of various types being destroyed, but some 30 of the attacking force were claimed shot down by British and US defences.

The increasingly desperate war situation also added an unusual twist to the story of the Ju 88G's already varied operational record. Some examples of the type were used, late in the war, as makeshift bombers and munitions transports.

The increasing importance of the Luftwaffe's day/night fighter force was demonstrated late in World War Two with the re-training of bomber crew members as fighter pilots. Several of the increasingly redundant bomber units were re-designated as KG(J) fighter units, there being a far greater need for fighter pilots to defend the Third Reich and its crumbling defences.

This applied not just to conversion onto day fighters to combat USAAF daytime air raids. The 3rd Gruppe of the long-standing bomber wing KG 2, for example, was earmarked for conversion onto Ju 88G night fighters (and the enigmatic Dornier Do 335), and some examples of the Ju 88 found their way to this unit before it was disbanded during March 1945.

In the closing days of the war, a desperate situation had developed for German forces in the so-called Courland Pocket (Latvia). Surrounded by Soviet forces, the only possible

escape was by air. An evacuation was launched on May 8, employing a variety of Luftwaffe assets based in Norway, including Ju 188A-3 torpedo bombers of III./KG 26, and various other aircraft including several Ju 88G-6 night fighters of 4./NJG 3. Only one of the night fighters managed to survive the makeshift operation, reaching Kiel-Holtenau airfield with several rescued personnel aboard. This was quite probably the last flight during World War Two of the once proud and powerful Luftwaffe night fighter force. ◾

This apparently brand-new Ju 88G-6 was captured at Langensalza, a Junkers facility associated with the major company factory at Bernburg. The aircraft was WNr 623185. Its nose radar array for the FuG 220 featured angled dipoles… apparently to better avoid interference.

EIGHTY-EIGHT EXPERTEN

The Junkers Ju 88 enabled various pilots to gain fame through Germany's propaganda system

The most celebrated Ju 88 bomber pilot was Werner Baumbach of KG 30, seen here with a Ju 88A in the background. He wears the muted yellow-coloured early style life preserver, vital for flights over water. (Malcolm V Lowe Collection)

Heinrich Prinz zu Sayn-Wittgenstein beside the tailplane of a Ju 88 night fighter, adorned with victory symbols. As a member of German nobility, and a prized asset of the Nachtjagd force, his death during January 1944 was a severe blow to the Luftwaffe. (John Batchelor Collection)

G ermany's Ju 88 was undoubtedly one of the Nazis' principal warplanes of World War Two, and as such, several Luftwaffe personalities were involved with its operations.

Bomber pilots generally never matched their fighter counterparts in the publicity stakes, especially due to the attentions of the Press. Nevertheless, several bomber flyers who called the Ju 88 home did receive fame. Among them was Werner Baumbach, one of the true 'bomber aces' of World War Two. An exponent of the Ju 88 from the type's initial testing, he flew the aircraft with KG 30 during the early wartime campaigns. He became something of a 'pin-up' in the German media and was much photographed, his anti-shipping successes being particularly lauded. Later in the war he became involved heavily with the unorthodox Mistel composite aircraft programme, and rose to be the Geschwader Kommodore of the special operations unit KG 200. Following the war, Baumbach eventually moved to Argentina, South America. Tragically, after surviving numerous perilous combat missions during World War Two, he was killed there in, ironically, the crash of an Avro Lancaster.

Junkers' own test pilots were especially celebrated due to the achievement of the Ju 88V5 in breaking a world record during March 1939, prior to the outbreak of the war. The successful flight was made by Ernst Seibert and Kurt Heintz (their names were often spelled alternatively in the press and media of the time as Siebert and Heinz). Flying in a closed circuit between Dessau and the Zugspitze mountain in Bavaria, and back to Dessau, a distance of 621 miles (1,000km) with a 4,409lb (2,000kg) payload, they covered the distance in 116 minutes at an average speed of 321.25mph (517km/h). This success ensured the two pilots, and the Ju 88, received international acclaim, and newspapers across Europe carried the news.

An important German aviator who also flew the Ju 88 for the Junkers company was Richard Perlia, who was also a test pilot for rotorcraft pioneer Flettner…and flew many early helicopters for that organisation.

decorated exponent of the Ju 88 and eventually rose to be Geschwader Kommodore of NJG 2. The exploits of the Luftwaffe's night fighter pilots were reported widely in Nazi Germany, partly as a morale boost while the Allied bombing campaign gained intensity, and Sayn-Wittgenstein became well known. Although not all his victories were achieved in the Ju 88, he flew the type successfully with his crew on many occasions. He was shot down and killed during the evening of January 21, 1944, it is believed by a de Havilland Mosquito night fighter of 141 Squadron RAF, which was using Serrate detection and homing gear for locating and tracking radar-equipped German night fighters. ◖▬

A retouched but nonetheless interesting image of the record-breaking combination of the two Junkers pilots, Kurt Heintz (or Heinz) on the right, standing beside the Ju 88V5, following their record-breaking flight of March 1939. Images such as this were duly used in Junkers publicity material. (Junkers)

Flying the Ju 88 certainly did not do this well-travelled pilot any harm, because he lived to be more than 100 years old.

Combat success

Undoubtedly the best-known among the Ju 88's crews were those of the Luftwaffe night fighter force, several of whom became high-scoring 'aces'. Among them was the celebrated Major Heinrich Prinz zu Sayn-Wittgenstein, who overall was the third highest-scoring Luftwaffe night fighter pilot. Credited with 83 aerial victories, he was a highly

Hans-Joachim 'Hajo' Herrmann received the Knight's Cross with Oak Leaves and Swords, some of these decorations for his Ju 88 exploits. One of these was his attack on the ammunition ship SS *Clan Fraser;* the resulting explosion sank 11 ships and made the port of Piraeus, Greece, unusable for many weeks. (Chris Clifford Collection)

Several Ju 88 personalities photographed at Dessau. Junkers 'top brass' include Ernst Zindel (far left) and Heinrich Hertel (far right). Beside Zindel is test pilot Karl-Heinz Kindermann, who flew the Ju 88V1 on its first flight in December 1936. Famous Luftwaffe Ju 88 pilot Werner Baumbach is fifth from the right. (via Peter Walter)

MUD-MOVING DEVELOPMENT

Illustrating its versatility, the Ju 88 was developed into several ground-attack derivatives based on initial Ju 88A 'schnellbomber' production versions

The success of the basic Ju 88A bomber layout led Junkers' designers to develop a number of closely related versions, derived from the original series-production medium bomber configuration. This resulted initially in the creation of a whole family of Ju 88 sub-types, which stemmed particularly from the A-5 and then the later A-4 layout. As described earlier in this book, the latter followed the first production frontline Ju 88A models, the A-1 and A-5.

The Ju 88A family eventually ran to 17 recognised or intended production/ conversion sub-types and marks. Alongside the initial versions in the 'A' line, several of these later models also served in combat with the Luftwaffe, in bomber and close-support roles.

▶ An apparently retouched (but nonetheless interesting) image of a Ju 88A-6, fitted with the cumbersome barrage balloon cable-cutting equipment. Although in theory a good idea, in practice the framework degraded performance and survivability.

Sometimes misidentified as a Ju 88A-6/U maritime reconnaissance aircraft, this aircraft's werk nummer shows it was in fact an A-4… although the configuration of FuG 200 Hohentwiel radar aerials on its nose was similar to the A-6/U layout.

The Ju 88A-14 was arguably the best of the A-series bombers. This aircraft, variously described as a late-production A-4 or genuinely an A-14, illustrates increased forward armament and the clean, classic lines of the type. (All Malcolm V Lowe Collection unless stated)

Once again, this underlined the 1930s thinking of the Nazi hierarchy, that light/medium bombers of the Luftwaffe were for use in a short-/medium-range tactical capacity – in line with the philosophy that longer-range strategic heavy bombers were not vitally important.

Cable cutters

Numerically, the Ju 88A-6 was the next major version following the A-5 and A-4. It was based on the former, and featured a cumbersome external framework attached to the forward fuselage and outer wing panels, for cutting barrage balloon cables ahead of main force bombers. Although this was an important necessity, especially as balloon barrages over England were

effective during the Battle of Britain, the ungainly device created drag and made the A-6's performance very poor; the concept was eventually abandoned. Aircraft so fitted were identifiable by the mountings for the framework on the forward fuselage, visible even when the frame was not installed. The process was also undertaken in the Ju 88A-8, thought to be based on the A-4's airframe. However, separately and far more successfully, several methods were attempted to guard normal Ju 88A bombers against the potentially lethal barrage balloon cables, including cable cutters installed onto part of the prominent nose framework…the so-called (and heavily glazed) 'beetle's eye' front fuselage of the Ju 88A-series bombers. These did not create drag or reduce performance unduly.

An oddball spin-off from the Ju 88A-6 programme was the A-6/U. This unique model was intended for maritime patrol and, to accommodate extra fuel, the crew was reduced to three and the ventral gondola was removed. Instead, FuG 200 'Hohentwiel' sea-search radar was installed, with prominent aerials attached to the nose/forward fuselage. Large long-range fuel tanks were mounted on external underwing pylons inboard of the engine nacelles, one on each side, and power came from two Jumo 211J engines (usually fitted to the Ju 88A-4).

With the increasing use of Ju 88As in desert conditions, as in North Africa and the hot and dusty Russian summer climate, modifications were carried out to allow the Ju 88A-series to operate successfully in this »

Many examples of the Ju 88A-6 had the cumbersome barrage balloon cable-cutting framework removed and reverted to being normal bombers. The fittings for the device remained visible, as seen here just ahead of the cockpit on this airframe possibly operated by KG 30. (via Peter Walter)

► The Ju 88A series included many armament options and alterations. Some were factory-applied, others being field conversion sets, while several were ad hoc, such as this unusual revised gondola on a Ju 88A-5, with twin 20mm MG FF cannons.

► The LT (Luft Torpedo) F5b was a major air-launched weapon in the Lutftwaffe's inventory. Those carried by Ju 88s, including the specialist anti-shipping A-17 model, usually had stabilising fins (not shown here) to steady the munition prior to it reaching the water/on entry.

► To assist take-off for heavily laden aircraft, some Ju 88s were fitted with rocket packs, one beneath each outer wing section. Known as 'Rauchgeräte', these units were very effective but often in short supply.

challenging environment. Alterations were mainly on the interior and were not visible, including special filters for the engine-related intakes, and survival equipment for the crew. The conversions to existing airframes were prefixed with the abbreviation '/Trop' (for example, Ju 88A-4/Trop), but several designations were reserved for upgrades planned or actually taking place on the production line; A-9 for the A-1, A-10 for the A-5, and A-11 for the tropicalised A-4.

Major developments

The most important specifically related derivative of the Ju 88A-4 was the A-14. Although the former is sometimes regarded as the definitive A-series production model, the latter was a significant improvement, based partly on combat experience with early production versions of the Ju

88A family, including the A-4 itself.

One of the important additions to the airframe was provision for a forward-firing 20mm MG FF cannon to repel frontal attacks from fighters, and to ensure useful additional air-to-ground firepower. This installation had already been tried, sometimes as a field modification, before its adoption in A-14 production aircraft. The exact location had varied on earlier airframes, and some were retrofitted with the new equipment,

which eliminated the bomb-aimer's sloping oval window at the front of the lower fuselage gondola, with a chute for ejecting spent cartridges. As with other armament variations on the Ju 88A series, different equipment fits were apparent on the A-14, although it is generally regarded that this sub-type was the best of the A-series bombers. It is now generally accepted it also featured, as standard, a re-designed wing leading edge for balloon cable cutting. This so-called 'Kuto-Nase' installation was possibly trialled on the earlier Ju 88A-8 version.

A rather unconventional member of the family was the A-13, which was an A-4 intended specifically for close-support and anti-personnel operations. With dive brakes and other normal bombing equipment removed, but toting additional armour-plating for the crew and sensitive parts of the airframe, it was equipped with anti-personnel fragmentation bombs, and additional gun pods carried on the external underwing bomb carriers/pylons inboard of the engine nacelles.

Among the later marks of A-series production, an important model was the A-17. This was also the highest-numbered Ju 88A sub-type to be series built, and was a dedicated torpedo-carrying derivative. Weapons qualification was carried out at the test station at Tarnewitz, although pre-dating this version were several standard Ju 88A-4 airframes converted to carry torpedoes (and sometimes called Ju 88A-4/Torp). Among the alterations to the basic layout to create the dedicated A-17 anti-shipping version, was deletion of the ventral gondola, and the removal of two external underwing bomb carriers/pylons inboard of the engine nacelles; in their place was one special PVC carrier for a torpedo, the type most often associated with the A-17 was an LT F5b of some 1,653lb

(750kg). The type could therefore normally carry two torpedoes, and had a nominal crew of three. Weapons aiming and guidance was by means of equipment housed in a fairing on the starboard side of the forward fuselage. Power came via two Jumo 211J engines. This version flew operationally, although carriage of the two large torpedoes degraded performance considerably.

To increase the Ju 88A's capability as a tactical bomber, and especially to place as much weaponry as possible inside the fuselage, the Ju 88A-15 was developed from the A-4. Generally, a feature of the bomber marks of the A-series was most of the bombs were carried externally, thus creating much drag. Junkers' designers therefore considered increasing the type's existing (comparatively limited) internal bomb-carrying capability. The small bomb bay of the standard production Ju 88A bombers was therefore enlarged substantially, with a wooden bulbous extension beneath the fuselage, as tested on the Ju 88V60, coded SL+PC. This allowed a maximum of 6,614lb (3,000kg) of weapons to be carried. However, it did not become standard for Ju 88A-series bombers, and the A-15 version did not enter production… but the concept made a reappearance on the Ju 388.

Training needs

Among the A-series versions, a number of training derivatives were built specifically to school potential

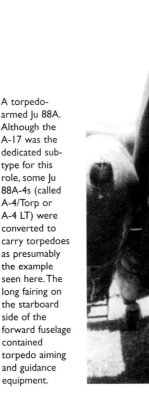

Various heavy anti-tank weapons were tested for possible use by the Ju 88P series of tank hunters. The installation of a 75mm gun caused damage to this aircraft's propellers during testing. (John Batchelor Collection)

A torpedo-armed Ju 88A. Although the A-17 was the dedicated sub-type for this role, some Ju 88A-4s (called A-4/Torp or A-4 LT) were converted to carry torpedoes as presumably the example seen here. The long fairing on the starboard side of the forward fuselage contained torpedo aiming and guidance equipment.

pilots on the type. However, turning the basic layout into this conversion training configuration was challenging. An important feature of the whole

Ju 88 family was the rather cramped forward fuselage crew compartment, where all personnel sat. This made converting the basic layout of the type for tuition into a difficult process. In the event, several training versions of the Ju 88 existed and, although they were dual-control machines, the instructor had just rudimentary auxiliary controls and instruments due to space considerations. However, particularly in the early part of the war, trainee pilots were already experienced on multi-engine types from training schools, so their conversion onto the Ju 88A was comparatively straightforward – although the dive-bombing characteristics and combat capability of the type, of course, had to be mastered as well.

The initial training version within the Ju 88A-series was the A-3, which was linked closely to the early operational A-1 bomber. It was ❯❯

The Ju 88S-series airframes featured a completely altered lower forward fuselage, replacing the Ju 88A's prominent gondola with the revised crew entrance hatch seen here – and a small fairing for the type's Lotfe bomb sight. (via Peter Walter)

(Bordkanone) 3.7cm cannon mounted in a pod beneath each wing. The Henschel Hs 129B was also developed for this task, with a single 3cm anti-tank cannon mounted in a fairing beneath the fuselage. Junkers' designers worked on a possible '88 derivative for the same role, and a Ju 88A was used as a development aircraft for this task. The result was the Ju 88P, although this version existed just in small numbers. Initial flight testing commenced with a converted Ju 88A, designated as the Ju 88V52 development aircraft. In the event, several Ju 88A airframes were converted to 'P' configuration, the designations P-1 to P-4 being employed for various weapons

A brand new and apparently early production Ju 88S-1 awaits delivery. It shows the clean and elegant lines of this fast version of the Ju 88 bomber family, with its neatly contoured 'glass' nose.

Several different muzzle brake designs were tested for the Ju 88P-1 'tank killer', until the design seen here was adopted for the type's 75mm anti-tank gun. (John Batchelor Collection)

followed by the A-7, a training variant associated with the later A-5. Two further dedicated instructional models in the Ju 88A line were created, the A-12 and A-16. The former was a further refined model, some reputably modified from Ju 88A-4 bombers, with the ventral gondola and dive brakes removed (although this apparently also applied to some of the previous trainers). The A-16 is usually referred to as a training variant linked to the A-14 bomber.

In addition, examples of war-weary former Ju 88s were retired to multi-engine flying schools, when their operational careers had come to an end. In total, the Ju 88 (as a whole) soldiered on in the training role right to the final weeks of the war. Among the many wrecked Ju 88s captured by the Allies at the end of the war in Europe, during May 1945, were many operational and non-operational Ju 88s, the latter including training machines.

Flying artillery

An offshoot from the A-series was the little-known Ju 88P. This dedicated attack aircraft was designed primarily as a tank-buster, although with other possible roles such as anti-shipping. On the Eastern Front, Junkers' Ju 87G Stuka was proving important in the anti-armour role against Soviet tanks such as the T-34, with a BK

installations, with heavy cannons in an under-fuselage fairing. The most distinctive of these was a planned addition to the P-1, of a long-barrelled 75mm PaK 40 cannon. A further distinctive feature of the Ju 88P was the 'solid' nose of the type, which was similar to the Ju 88C-series, rather than the heavily glazed 'beetle's eye' of the standard A-series bombers.

Speedy 'Siegfried'

Although designed originally as a 'schnellbomber', by the latter half of 1942, it was becoming clear the Ju 88A's performance was falling behind that of opposing fighters, which were proving increasingly successful against the type…especially over the Soviet Union. Junkers' designers already had in mind potential improvements of the basic Ju 88 layout, and these included a different choice of powerplant. The result was the fast, stripped-down, BMW 801-powered Ju 88S.

'Siegfried' was in fact a radical re-design of the standard Ju 88A-4. The latter had introduced more armour protection for the forward fuselage crew compartment, compared to previous marks, but this was reduced in the S-series to decrease weight. The lower fuselage gondola was removed, and

a completely new glazed nose was introduced. This was more streamlined than the beetle's eye of the A-series, and resembled the neatly contoured nose outline of the early Ju 88 prototype/development aircraft. The external underwing bomb carriers/pylons inboard of the engine nacelles (two under each wing of Ju 88A-series aircraft) were replaced by a single weapons station each side, which could carry a bomb of up to 2,205lb (1,000kg).

Development work fell to a converted Ju 88A-4, the Ju 88V55, which first flew in this guise during December 1942. An initial batch of Ju 88S-0 pre-production examples was followed by the Ju 88S-1 initial production, this version being powered by the BMW 801G/G-2 engine, which had GM-1 nitrous oxide power boost, with a special

emergency setting, and a power rating of 1,700/1,730hp at 5,000ft (1,524m). This gave a very credible top speed, with boost, that Junkers claimed to be 379mph (610km/h) at 26,247ft (8,000m), making the S-series the fastest of the Ju 88 bomber line. Defensive armament, however, was limited to one flexible-mounted MG 131 machine gun, firing rearwards from the crew compartment.

Also BMW 801-powered was the Ju 88S-2, but the S-3 reverted to Junkers Jumo engines, in this case the 213A bomber engine with GM-1 boost. However, never numerous, approximately just 200 Ju 88S-series aircraft were manufactured/converted.

A further bomber mark of the Ju 88 family existed, the Ju 88B, but development of this distinctively different derivative led to the Ju 188, which is described separately.

CLOSING THE CIRCLE

Bomber versions of the Ju 88 became operational on all
fronts as the war progressed, confirming the type as one
of the Luftwaffe's most important combat aircraft

A very large
bomb being
manhandled
ingeniously
for installation
on a Ju 88A-4
(M2+AK) of
KGr 106, which
was one of
the original
coastal groups
that eventually
became fully
fledged bomber
units.

During the Battle of Britain the Ju 88A was a vital asset in the Luftwaffe's bombing campaign, even though losses had been high.

Ultimately, the failure of the Luftwaffe's actions during the Battle of Britain had led to the nocturnal Blitz on Britain, which progressed from later in 1940 into 1941, and was followed by sporadic but nonetheless deadly attacks against Britain during the following years.

However, with the war expanding continually to other fronts, 1941

brought a major change in the deployment and tactics for the Luftwaffe's bomber force. The new Ju 88A-4 was at the forefront of these actions. To begin with, flights over the British Isles were curbed significantly. The main reason for this migration of Ju 88 units away from the West (and their operations as a part of, or associated with Luftflotte 3), was the impending German attack on the Soviet Union. Before that time, though, the Germans became embroiled in remedying a mess

in which the Italians had become embroiled, with a failed attack on Greece, and in the expanding air war in the Mediterranean.

The Ju 88A was involved in Operation Marita, the German attack on Greece during April 1941, which also widened to include operations against Yugoslavia. Significant among the units involved was LG 1, and this geschwader became something of an institution in the Mediterranean and Southern Europe thenceforward, until 1944. North Africa was another area in which the Germans had to intervene on behalf of the increasingly hard-pressed Italians, and this expanded to significant operations there throughout 1942 and the first half of 1943, with major attacks on the fortress island of Malta included. The Ju 88A was well to the fore in these sorties, with several Ju 88A units being additional to elements of LG 1.

As part of the operations in the Mediterranean, anti-shipping strikes by Ju 88s became important. They included not just the use of dedicated torpedo-carrying Ju 88A-4/Torp and Ju 88A-17 aircraft, but conventional horizontal and dive bombing against

One of a sequence of images taken of the attractive Wellenmuster (wave pattern)-camouflaged Ju 88A-4 from I./ KG 54, coded B3+MH, which landed at Dübendorf airfield in Switzerland during October 1943. It subsequently wore Swiss markings for a time. (via John Batchelor)

and major surface forces, Norwegian-based Ju 88A bombers and torpedo bombers were a major thorn in the side of the Arctic Convoys to the northern Russian ports. Significant attacks were made on Convoy PQ 16 and found their most infamous result in the major and very successful operations against PQ 17.

Major offensive

By the summer of 1941, several bomber units formerly equipped with the Dornier Do 17 were upgrading to the Ju 88A. With a few exceptions, most German bomber units were flying the He 111 and Ju 88 by the start of Operation Barbarossa, the hugely important German attack on the Soviet Union. The Ju 88 became a capable and valuable asset to the Luftwaffe over what became, from June 22, 1941 onwards, the Eastern Front. From the first day of operations against Soviet forces, Ju 88A units enjoyed considerable success, attacking enemy airfields at low level and causing staggering losses among Soviet bomber and fighter units. Several of the Ju 88A geschwader, including KG 3 and KG 51, achieved enormous fortune in this role. Nevertheless, the Ju 88As also suffered important losses with 23 documented by the Germans as destroyed, by the end of the campaign's first day. III./KG 51's bombing of the airfield at Kurovitsy/ Siversky was typical; although successfully catching many Soviet aircraft on the ground, six Ju 88As were shot down by defending fighters. Further north, KG 1's Ju 88As caused havoc with attacks on several airfields,

which during the first week of the campaign, weakened Soviet airpower considerably in the northern sector of the German operations.

The Ju 88s were employed additionally in the ground support role, allowing German Panzer forces to push forward relentlessly in this initial, highly successful part of the invasion. This resulted, however, in severe losses from ground fire. Turning their attention more and more to the ground war, having gained air superiority, the Ju 88As were often used in the dive-bombing role. On July 1, for example, the Junkers of KG 51 and KG 54 helped to fend off a Soviet counter-attack by bombing tanks and other terrestrial assets. Soviet supply lines and communications, including rail and road links, and bridges, were all attacked with overwhelming ⏩

This classic view looking towards the rear of a Ju 88A, probably an A-4, shows the arrangement of the underwing bomb carriers/ pylons and offset gondola, with its bomb-aimer's window and Lotfe bomb sight fitting. (all Malcolm V Lowe Collection unless stated)

Allied shipping. The Malta Convoys became a significant target during 1942, in addition to attacks on Malta itself. Several kampfgeschwader operated torpedo-bomber Ju 88As, including notably KG 26 and KG 77. Mining operations were also flown.

The scope of Ju 88 anti-shipping work widened to operations in much colder climes, as the significance of the seaborne supply route to the Soviet Union from northern British ports grew steadily. In addition to U-boats

A groundcrew member has unwisely fallen asleep beside a stockpile of bombs in the Russian snow, with a Ju 88A-5 of KG 1 in the background. KG 1's Ju 88A fleet caused havoc among the Soviet forces in the early days of the German invasion during June and July 1941.

A propaganda image intended to show how well equipped and prepared the Germans were to survive in the Soviet winter which, in reality, shows how difficult the conditions were for man and machine. The aircraft is a Ju 88A. (via Peter Walter)

initial success.

Nevertheless, the failure of the German forces to win the war against the Soviet Union during those first few weeks and months of the campaign led to what eventually became a disastrous war of attrition. The terrible Russian winter took a massive toll on German manpower and equipment, with flying operations affected in turn. Subsequently, the Ju 88A force was involved in all major actions on the Eastern Front, including such calamitous operations as the Stalingrad fighting during late 1942 and early 1943, and Kursk in July-August 1943.

Continuing Blitz

It was not just in the Mediterranean/ North Africa and over the Soviet Union that the Ju 88 was in action during the mid- and later-war period. German bombing against the British Isles had continued, albeit with smaller numbers of aircraft, from 1941 onwards and Ju 88s were also involved in the maritime war over the Atlantic.

Reassignment of Luftwaffe bomber units to Eastern and Southern Europe during 1941 had produced a slackening (but never a cessation) of aerial attacks against Britain. Elements of KG 30 alone had remained as the chief instigator of Ju 88 raids on the British Isles. However, attacks against Britain resumed on a much larger scale during 1942. The RAF bombing of Lübeck during the night of March 28-29, 1942 in which civilian areas and

A small crane is used to manhandle a torpedo, while a Ju 88A waits in the background. The LT F5b torpedo weighed approximately 1,653lb (750kg), and did nothing positive for the carrying aircraft's aerodynamics until it was released.

the historic old town were targeted deliberately with disastrous results for the local population and infrastructure, brought about a furious reaction from Nazi leadership. Thenceforth, similarly historic British towns and cities and

their civilian populations were to be targeted, in what became known infamously as the so-called Baedeker Blitz or Baedeker raids.

The Baedeker Guides were travel books published by the German company Karl Baedeker from the 1830s onwards. Included in them were details of historic British towns, some of which were duly selected to become targets for retaliatory raids in response to the RAF bombing of Lübeck and later other German towns and cities. Most of those targeted had little or no military value, but were chosen for their cultural and historical significance, which represented another switch from a central purpose of the Ju 88's original creation, that of tactical support for German ground forces. The main series of raids began during late April 1942, and ended by the end of May, though towns and cities continued to be targeted for their cultural value for the next two years.

The task of prosecuting the attacks fell to bomber groups of Luftflotte

3. This organisation had been fully involved in Battle of France and Battle of Britain operations, but had been reduced in numbers considerably due to increasing combat requirements from other theatres. Thus, Ju 88A units that duly participated in the Baedeker raids were a mixed bag from several geschwader brought in specially for these attacks. Involved were elements of KG 3 and KG 77, with the inevitable KG 30 also participating. Kampfgruppe (KGr) 106, a former coastal unit that had converted onto the Ju 88A, was also included. The first raid of the Baedeker Blitz was directed against Exeter, on the night of April 23-24, 1942. For several weeks these mainly after-dark raids were pursued with intensity, each in theory involving 30 to 40 aircraft, and to increase their effectiveness it was planned for each crew to fly two sorties per night. Each raid would involve two periods of 60 to 90 minutes, separated by two or three hours. The campaign began to falter though, as more units were needed to bolster Luftwaffe operations elsewhere; British defences (especially at night) became more efficient, and units on the Eastern Front began to receive priority for new aircraft. Nonetheless, the attacks continued during 1943, albeit bolstered by the fast low-level daytime hit-and-run Focke-Wulf Fw 190 fighter-bombers of SKG 10.

Eventually the Baedeker raids ceased in 1944, with unsustainable losses being suffered for no material or military gain. Instead, January 1944 brought a switch back to London as the principal

Ju 88s took a steady toll of Allied shipping, both warships and merchant vessels. This 'Anton' of 7./KG 30 had an impressive scoreboard on its vertical tail, a location often favoured for such individual tallies.

The long fairing along the starboard forward fuselage side identifies this aircraft as a Ju 88A-17 torpedo bomber. It probably belonged to KG 77 as the location is thought to be a Mediterranean airfield, probably in Italy during late 1943 or early 1944.
(John Batchelor Collection)

target for retaliation. On January 21 the Luftwaffe launched Operation Steinbock, which began with an all-out night attack on London, employing most of its available bomber force in the West. Again Luftflotte 3 was fully involved, and Steinbock proved to be the last strategic air offensive by the German bomber arm during the conflict. It is sometimes referred to as the 'Baby Blitz'. Raids were also flown against other targets largely in the south of England, and again Ju 88s were involved. This time, however, the Ju 88S had joined the 'Anton' force, as had the Ju 188. Steinbock was also largely a failure, though, with heavy losses for little or no military gain. Henceforth, from May 1944 onwards the Luftwaffe's efforts had to be re-directed toward English Channel ports the Germans suspected were going to be used for the inevitable

Allied invasion of Continental Europe. Ju 88s and Ju 188s participated in what became the last major raid on London by conventional aircraft, during the night of April 18-19, 1944; 125 aeroplanes were dispatched, but around just one half were effective, and 13 bombers were lost. In a major switch of emphasis and technology, aerial attacks on London became the preserve of Germany's V-weapons.

Elements of KG 54 were among the Ju 88 units involved in the Luftwaffe's often chaotic response to the D-Day landings of June 6, 1944, but lost five Ju 88s in an abortive attack on the British forces at 'Sword' beach on the evening of the first day. KG 6 was also involved in the post-invasion response, as was the ever-busy KG 30, but all Luftwaffe units suffered significant losses during this period.

Ju 88s were similarly involved in action against the Allied landings in southern France (Operation Dragoon) which began on August 15, 1944. Included were Ju 88As of II./KG 26, which was adapting its aircraft for conventional bombing, having all but relinquished its torpedo strike role. A number of sorties were flown against Allied troops on the landing beaches with some success, but the small number of aircraft involved rendered the Luftwaffe's response largely fruitless, II./KG 26 itself being withdrawn to Germany a short time later.

On January 1, 1945, the Luftwaffe carried out Operation Bodenplatte, a massive attack on Allied airfields on the Continent. This action mainly ⟫

The Versuchs-kommando für Panzerbe-kämpfung (anti-tank operational trials unit) briefly operated the Ju 88P-1 with its massive 75mm gun during April 1943 on the Eastern Front, including this aircraft bearing the unit's badge beneath the cockpit. (via Peter Walter)

involved fighters flying as ground-attack aircraft, as explained elsewhere in this book, with bombers or night fighters acting as their pathfinders. Ju 88s of various marks were involved in this largely fruitless operation.

Ju 88P specialist ground-attack aircraft existed purely in small numbers, but did serve operationally. The most impressive of the breed was the P-1 with its 75mm long-barrelled gun for anti-tank/anti-shipping work. The type was tested under operational conditions on the Eastern Front by the Versuchskommando für Panzerbekämpfung during April 1943, but did not prove particularly good

at its anti-tank role. Some examples might have served later with III./KG 1. The Ju 88P-3, with two BK 3.7cm cannons in a streamlined fairing beneath the fuselage, did somewhat better and it is often claimed this type was on the books of several night attack (Nachtschlachtgruppe) units.

Final operations

The Ju 88S series was the final expression of the family of bomber Ju 88s and, as such, was the type most prevalent in service from this line during the final months of the war. Two kampfgeschwader are mainly associated with this type, KG 6 and KG

66. Re-equipment with the Ju 88S-0 and S-1 began principally in the second half of 1943. III./KG 6, for example, was taken off operations and received its new arrivals during September and October 1943. It therefore participated in the opening Operation Steinbock raid against London on January 21, 1944, with the Ju 88S-1.

KG 66 had, as a part of its tasking, the specialist role of pathfinder target marking. I./KG 66 lost its first Ju 88S-1 near to the end of May 1943. Subsequently, it principally flew the Ju 188, but III./KG 66 went one better and flew the rare Ju 88S-3 later in 1944, and was intending to use this type as a pathfinder for Mistel operations if any had taken place against British targets.

By that time, however, the war position had turned irrevocably against the Luftwaffe. The situation became so dire for the Germans, with the Allies advancing on all fronts, that eventually aircraft based in the West could just as easily operate against Soviet forces in the East, so contracted was the German-held territory in some places by the war's end. However, by that time many of the bomber units had ceased to exist, or had been turned into fighter outfits. This was in response to the attempts to counter mass USAAF daylight bombing operations, but the plan to re-train bomber crew members as fighter pilots was largely unsuccessful. KG 6, for example, became KG(J) 6 during November 1944.

A classic head-on view of a Ju 88S-1, showing the type's neatly streamlined BMW 801 radial engine installation. This aircraft is believed to have flown with KG 66.

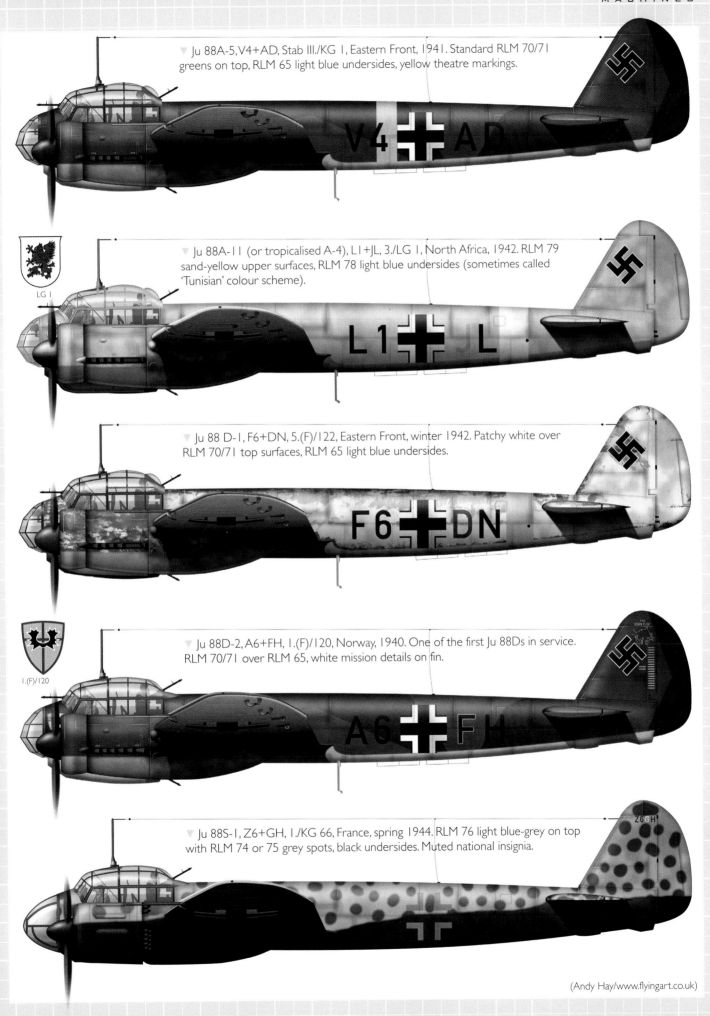

▼ Ju 88A-5, V4+AD, Stab III./KG 1, Eastern Front, 1941. Standard RLM 70/71 greens on top, RLM 65 light blue undersides, yellow theatre markings.

V4 + AD

LG 1

▼ Ju 88A-11 (or tropicalised A-4), L1+JL, 3./LG 1, North Africa, 1942. RLM 79 sand-yellow upper surfaces, RLM 78 light blue undersides (sometimes called 'Tunisian' colour scheme).

L1 + JL

▼ Ju 88 D-1, F6+DN, 5.(F)/122, Eastern Front, winter 1942. Patchy white over RLM 70/71 top surfaces, RLM 65 light blue undersides.

F6 + DN

I.(F)/120

▼ Ju 88D-2, A6+FH, I.(F)/120, Norway, 1940. One of the first Ju 88Ds in service. RLM 70/71 over RLM 65, white mission details on fin.

A6 + FH

▼ Ju 88S-1, Z6+GH, I./KG 66, France, spring 1944. RLM 76 light blue-grey on top with RLM 74 or 75 grey spots, black undersides. Muted national insignia.

(Andy Hay/www.flyingart.co.uk)

JUNKERS Ju 88G-1

1	Starboard navigation light	28	Control runs	52	Bulkhead
2	Wingtip profile	29	Pilot's armoured seat	53	Control linkage access plate
3	FuG 227 'Flensburg' radar receiver antenna	30	Sliding window section	54	Fuselage stringers
4	Starboard aileron	31	Headrest	55	Upper longeron
5	Aileron control runs	32	Jettisonable canopy roof section	56	Maintenance walkway
6	Starboard flaps	33	Gun restraint	57	Control linkage
7	Flap-fairing strip	34	Wireless operator/gunner's seat	58	Horizontal construction joint
8	Wing ribs	35	Rheinmetall Borsig MG 131 machine gun (13mm)	59	Z-section fuselage frames
9	Starboard outer fuel tank (415 lit/91 Imp gal)	36	Radio equipment (FuG 10P HF, FuG 16ZY VHF, FuG 25 IFF)	60	Dinghy stowage
10	Fuel filler cap			61	Fuel vent pipe
11	Leading edge structure	37	Ammunition box (500 rounds of 13mm)	62	Master compass
12	Annular exhaust slot	38	FuG 220 'Lichtenstein' SN-2 indicator box	63	Spherical oxygen bottles
13	Cylinder head fairings	39	FuG 227 'Flensburg' indicator box	64	Accumulator
14	Adjustable nacelle nose ring	40	Control linkage	65	Tailplane centre section carry-through
15	Twelve-blade cooling fan	41	Bulkhead	66	Starboard tailplane

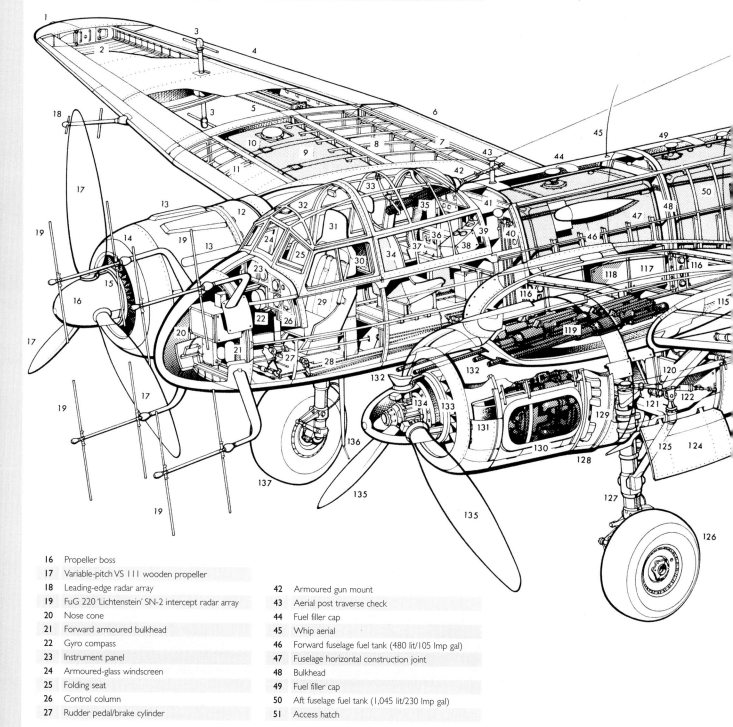

16	Propeller boss		
17	Variable-pitch VS 111 wooden propeller		
18	Leading-edge radar array	42	Armoured gun mount
19	FuG 220 'Lichtenstein' SN-2 intercept radar array	43	Aerial post traverse check
20	Nose cone	44	Fuel filler cap
21	Forward armoured bulkhead	45	Whip aerial
22	Gyro compass	46	Forward fuselage fuel tank (480 lit/105 Imp gal)
23	Instrument panel	47	Fuselage horizontal construction joint
24	Armoured-glass windscreen	48	Bulkhead
25	Folding seat	49	Fuel filler cap
26	Control column	50	Aft fuselage fuel tank (1,045 lit/230 Imp gal)
27	Rudder pedal/brake cylinder	51	Access hatch

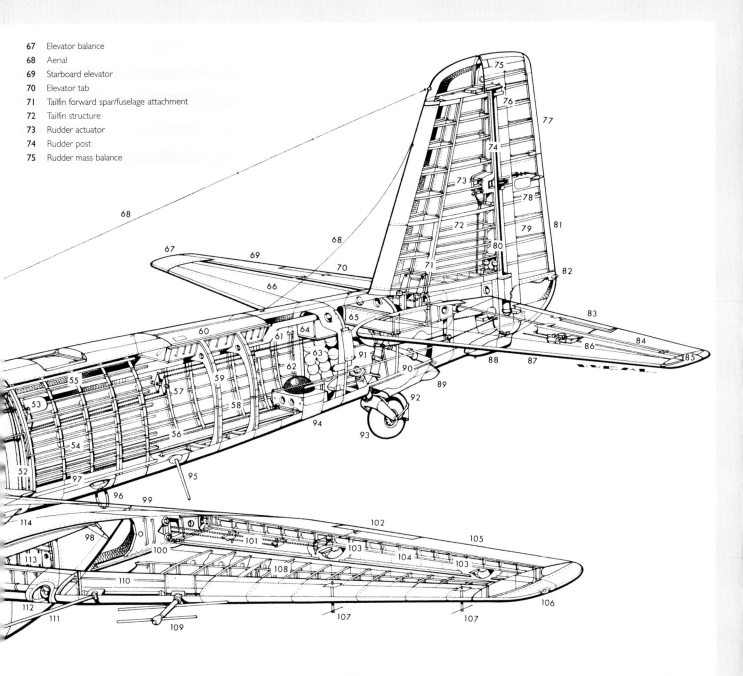

67 Elevator balance
68 Aerial
69 Starboard elevator
70 Elevator tab
71 Tailfin forward spar/fuselage attachment
72 Tailfin structure
73 Rudder actuator
74 Rudder post
75 Rudder mass balance

76 Rudder upper hinge
77 Rudder tab (upper section)
78 Inspection/maintenance handhold
79 Rudder structure
80 Tail fin aft spar/fuselage attachment
81 Rudder tab (lower section)
82 Rear navigation light
83 Elevator tab
84 Port elevator
85 Elevator balance
86 Elevator tab actuator
87 Heated leading edge
88 Tail bumper/fuel vent outlet
89 Tailwheel doors
90 Tailwheel retraction mechanism
91 Shock absorber leg
92 Mudguard
93 Tailwheel
94 Access hatch
95 Fixed antenna
96 D/F loop

97 Lower longeron
98 Nacelle/flap fairing
99 Port flap
100 Wing centre/outer section attachment point
101 Aileron controls
102 Aileron tab (port only)
103 Aileron hinges
104 Rear spar
105 Port aileron
106 Port navigation light
107 FuG 101a radio altimeter antenna
108 Wing structure
109 Leading-edge radar array
110 Forward spar
111 Pitot head
112 Landing lamp
113 Mainwheel well rear bulkhead
114 Port outer fuel tank location (415 lit/91 Imp gal)
115 Ventral gun pack (offset to port)
116 Ball-and-socket fuselage/wing attachment points
117 Port inner fuel tank location (425 lit/93.4 Imp gal)

118 Ammunition boxes for MG 151 cannon (200 rpg)
119 Mauser MG 151/20 cannon (four) of 20mm calibre
120 Mainwheel leg retraction yoke
121 Leg pivot member
122 Mainwheel door actuating jack
123 Mainwheel door (rear section)
124 Mainwheel door (forward section)
125 Leg support strut
126 Port mainwheel
127 Mainwheel leg
128 Annular exhaust slot
129 Exhaust stubs (internal)
130 BMW 801D air-cooled radial engine (partly omitted for clarity)
131 Annular oil tank
132 Cannon muzzles (depressed five degrees)
133 Twelve-blade cooling fan
134 Propeller mechanism
135 Variable-pitch wooden VS 111 propeller
136 FuG 16ZY antenna
137 Starboard mainwheel

D5+EV wears the classic Luftwaffe splinter pattern camouflage of RLM 70 and 71 over 65 undersides.

WALK AROUND

Relish the fine detail on show, in these close-up images of the Ju 88R-1 displayed at the RAF Museum Cosford, UK

The RAF Museum Cosford's Ju 88R-1, WNr 360043/ D5+EV, was on strength with IV./NJG 3 in Denmark, during May 1943 before it was flown to Scotland by its defecting pilot, Oblt Schmitt. It was studied intensively by scientists (mainly for its prized FuG 202 Lichtenstein BC radar), and test-flown by service/Royal Aircraft Establishment pilots, before being placed in storage. At some point, dummy radar antennas were manufactured as part of the restoration. It is one of just two Ju 88s extant in the world today. D5+EV, and many more Luftwaffe types, are displayed at the RAF Museum Cosford; more details can be found at www. rafmuseum.org.uk/cosford

▲ BMW 801A engine cowlings and exhaust stubs. (all photos Matthew Roberts)

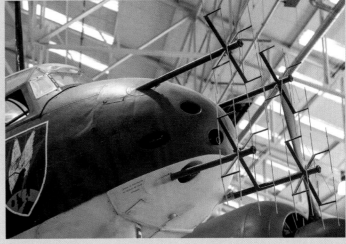

▲ Replica versions of the aircraft's original FuG 202 radar aerials.

▲ Single rear machine gun glazing/mount.

▲ Crew seats, and radio/radar boxes. Note the leather back pad on the pilot's seat.

▲ Starboard main undercarriage unit.

▶ The instrument panel has been just partially restored, but the control column and rudder pedals are visible.

◀ Mainwheel hub and tyre detail.

VIEW MORE ONLINE
www.airfixmodelworld.com

WALK AROUND

▲ Note the cooling fan blades, and BMW logo decorating the cowling ring.

▲ The bulge under the tail is the combined bumper and fuel vent outlet.

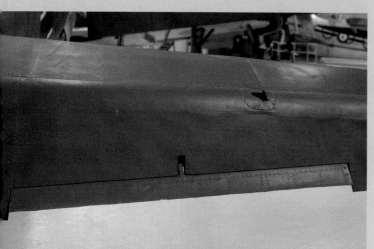

▲ The starboard elevator and trim tab.

▼ One of the main undercarriage bay doors, with characteristic lightening holes.

▲ Crew entry hatch to the rear of the undernose gondola.

▼ Tailwheel unit, here on a supporting display plinth.

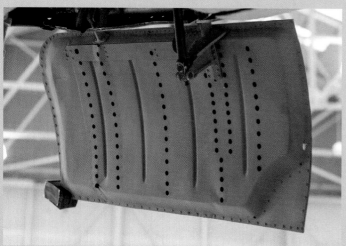

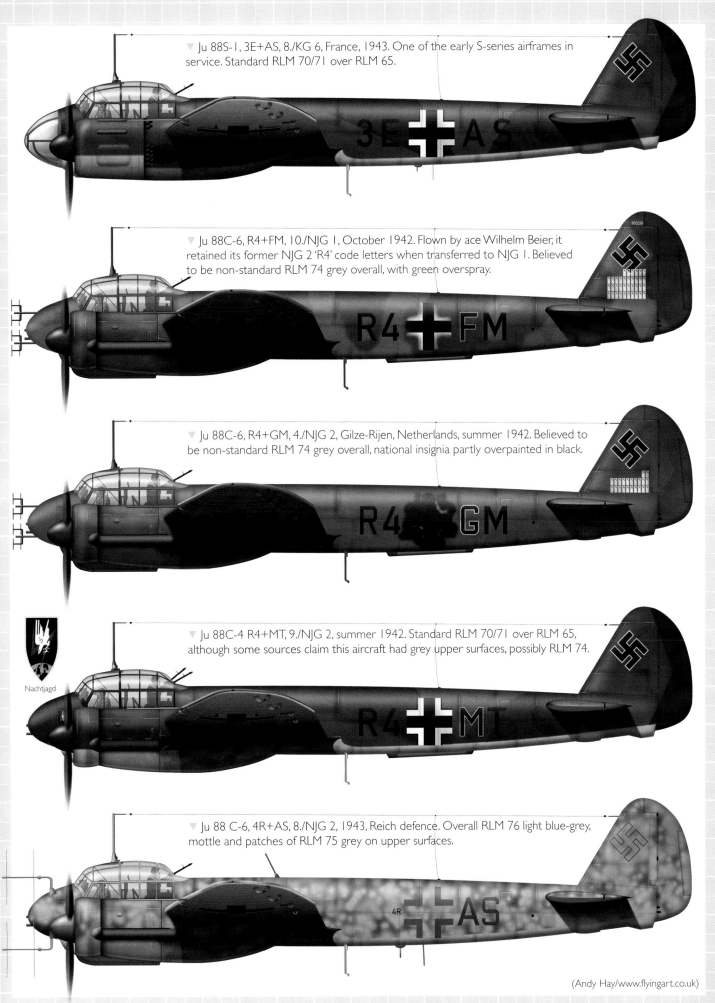

▽ Ju 88S-1, 3E+AS, 8./KG 6, France, 1943. One of the early S-series airframes in service. Standard RLM 70/71 over RLM 65.

▽ Ju 88C-6, R4+FM, 10./NJG 1, October 1942. Flown by ace Wilhelm Beier, it retained its former NJG 2 'R4' code letters when transferred to NJG 1. Believed to be non-standard RLM 74 grey overall, with green overspray.

▽ Ju 88C-6, R4+GM, 4./NJG 2, Gilze-Rijen, Netherlands, summer 1942. Believed to be non-standard RLM 74 grey overall, national insignia partly overpainted in black.

Nachtjagd

▽ Ju 88C-4 R4+MT, 9./NJG 2, summer 1942. Standard RLM 70/71 over RLM 65, although some sources claim this aircraft had grey upper surfaces, possibly RLM 74.

▽ Ju 88 C-6, 4R+AS, 8./NJG 2, 1943, Reich defence. Overall RLM 76 light blue-grey, mottle and patches of RLM 75 grey on upper surfaces.

(Andy Hay/www.flyingart.co.uk)

FLYING SPIES

Truly a versatile, multi-role aircraft, the Ju 88 was well suited to the highly specialised role of reconnaissance

One of the lesser-known operational duties of the Ju 88 was that of reconnaissance. This was a specific task the type performed exceptionally well, and several dedicated marks of Ju 88 were developed for the role. Indeed, reconnaissance versions of the type (initially) followed closely the development and production of bomber Ju 88s.

Overall, three distinct Ju 88 models were produced to execute recce. These were the basic Ju 88D, which was the most widespread variant and was linked closely to the major Ju 88A bomber series; the Ju 88T, which was a developed version later in the war related to the Ju 88S bomber; and the distinctive, long-fuselage and very rare Ju 88H.

Major production

The most important member of the line of recce Ju 88s, and certainly by far the most numerous, was the Ju 88D series. Early in the initial design phases of the Ju 88 programme, it had been obvious to Junkers' designers and management that the type could not just became an accomplished bomber, but was also a potential

Some early recce Ju 88A-1(F) and A-5(F) airframes were built new as such, rather than being converted from existing bombers. Here, new-build aircraft at Bernburg include an A-5(F) with the factory codes CD+OK nearest to the camera.

One of the earliest Ju 88s to be built as a reconnaissance version was this example, generally regarded to be the fifth Ju 88D-0 pre-production aircraft. It wore the factory codes (Stammkennzeichen) CB+OE. (All Malcolm V Lowe Collection unless stated)

Ju 88As were converted into recce platforms. These were from among the Ju 88A-1 and A-5 bombers then in service, the relevant conversions being referred to as Ju 88A-1(F) and Ju 88A-5(F)…the 'F' suffix standing for Fernaufklärung, or long-range recce. On these aircraft, the underwing dive brakes and external underwing bomb carriers/pylons inboard of the engine nacelles were removed, and the rear bomb bay was converted to house up to three cameras, with two circular optical 'windows' being installed in the starboard opening door, and one in the port. These openings allowed easy access to the cameras, while the forward bomb bay housed extra fuel.

Production of the first dedicated reconnaissance Ju 88s commenced during 1940, these being initially of the Ju 88D-0 pre-production series and D-2 production model. They were based on the Ju 88A-5 bomber, the latter being powered by Jumo 211G or H-series engines. On these newly manufactured aircraft the underwing bomb carriers/pylons were reinstated, for the carriage of external long-range fuel tanks.

Out of sequence numerically was the Ju 88D-1, which was based closely on the Ju 88A-4; echoing its bomber cousin, it leap-frogged later designations off the production line. This model incorporated all improvements the Ju 88A-4 introduced, in addition to its powerplant, but again with the

bombing equipment removed. In general, the wide variety of defensive armament variations that accompanied the bomber Ju 88As was similarly to be seen on all recce Ju 88Ds. The Ju 88D-1 was introduced during 1941, and was different to the preceding D-series aircraft in having its cameras mounted in a specially strengthened structure behind the rear bomb bay. Just two camera windows were fitted as standard, with the possibility ❯❯

▲ Aerial cameras of World War Two were bulky and heavy. Here, one of the larger German cameras, probably an Rb 75/30 as used in Ju 88 recce aircraft, is displayed by a Luftwaffe crewman.

basis for a recce platform as well. At that time, the rather ponderous but nonetheless useful Dornier Do 17P was a major type in the Luftwaffe's medium- to long-range recce inventory. The RLM and Luftwaffe soon identified the possibilities of the Ju 88 design as a potential camera-carrying aircraft, and early in the type's Luftwaffe career, several bomber

◄ A batch of Ju 88A-1(F) recce-configured aircraft was built at Bernburg, including this aircraft. Its camera windows can be seen on the lower fuselage surface, further back than the forward gondola.

Conditions in the Soviet winter were terrible for man and machine. This reconnaissance Ju 88D being dug out of the snow carried two underwing long-range fuel tanks.

Some recce aircraft carried bombs as well as defensive weapons, as shown by this Ju 88D-1/ Trop or D-3 in North Africa; its stores/ weapons carrier is marked with '1,000kg', its maximum carrying capacity. The entrance hatch to the gondola (C-Stand) has an MG 81Z (Z meaning 'zwilling' – twin) machine gun installation.

A number of publicity images were taken of recce Ju 88s operated by 5.(F)/122, on the Eastern Front during winter 1942-43. Included was this whitewashed Ju 88D-1 coded F6+DN.

to install a third as required. Usually carried was the Rb 75/30 camera for high-altitude work, and an Rb 50/30 for lower altitudes, or the Rb 20/30 for low-altitude coverage, depending on the requirements for a particular sortie. The cameras were operated remotely from the crew compartment, and were not accessible in flight. However, hand-held cameras could be used by crew members for additional photography if required. The installation of the cameras further aft on this version, though, resulted in the prominent 'towel rail' antenna carried by Ju 88s on the centre line of the lower fuselage being moved aft. The D-1's camera bay was heated, the vent for the petrol-fired warming equipment being mounted in a small fairing on the upper fuselage; a crew of four was normal.

In exactly the same way 'tropicalised' Ju 88A-series bombers were required due to the expanding envelope of Luftwaffe operations, which widened as war progressed, so recce versions of the Ju 88 needed similar protection. Improvements included the installation of air intake filters, and various survival equipment and food for the crew. This led to two further Ju 88D models, the D-3 (tropicalised version of the D-1), and the D-4 (a similarly upgraded derivative of the D-2). A number of existing D-1 aircraft were retrofitted as D-1/Trop, as were some D-2s, sometimes called D-2/Trop.

The final recognised version of the Ju 88D series was the Ju 88D-5. This model incorporated all the lessons

from the preceding models, and had a normal recce fit of three cameras, but this again could depend on mission profile. Most examples also featured narrow-chord VDM metal propellers (usually associated with earlier marks of Ju 88 bombers) rather than the broad-chord VS 11 wooden propeller blades of the Ju 88A-4 and associated marks. In addition to photographic and general surveillance missions, by day and night, Ju 88Ds were also used for the equally important role of weather reconnaissance.

Weather recce was another task carried out by the Ju 88. This D-1 coded 4T+GH belonged to Wekusta (Westa) 51, based in western France, for flights over the Bay of Biscay.

Higher performance

Although designed originally as a 'schnellbomber' able to out-run enemy fighters, by the latter half of 1942 it was becoming clear that the Ju 88A's performance was falling behind that of opposing fighters, which were proving increasingly successful against the type. The same was similarly also true for recce versions of the Ju 88, linked to the Ju 88A series, namely the Ju 88D. Junkers' designers duly made improvements to the basic Ju 88 layout, including a different choice of powerplant, and the result was the fast, stripped-down, BMW 801-powered Ju 88S. This new bomber version was

In-service images of genuine operational Ju 88T-series aircraft are tantalisingly rare. This is one of the few, showing a Ju 88T-1 coded 4U+MK of 2.(F)/123. The magazine containing film from one of the aircraft's cameras is in the hands of the man on the right.

significant in terms of recce-configured Ju 88s, because a new example of the latter incorporated improvements seen on the Ju 88S series; this new variant was designated Ju 88T.

Built in comparatively small numbers, in two main and distinct versions, the Ju 88T was the fastest and arguably the best of the recce-configured Ju 88s. The initial prototype/development Ju 88 for the planned 'S' bomber series, the Ju 88V55, first flew during December 1942, and work on the Ju 88T layout was pursued in the early months of 1943. It appears the small numbers of the initial production version, the Ju 88T-1, were either new-built, or probably mainly converted from existing Ju 88S-1s, the two being very similar except for the equipment fits for their very different mission profiles. The powerplant and boost system for the T-1 was therefore the same as the Ju 88S-1, with extra capacity for GM-1 nitrous oxide contained in a part of the internal bomb bay; similarly, the lower fuselage gondola of the earlier Ju 88s was removed as in the S-series. Also omitted was the small lower forward fuselage fairing of the Ju 88S that

housed the type's bombsight. Instead, various cameras could be carried in the fuselage, depending on mission requirements, as in the earlier Ju 88D series. A crew of three was carried, and defensive armament was usually limited to one flexible-mounted MG 131 machine gun in the rear of the cockpit glazing pointing aft (B-Stand), although this was apparently replaced with the more effective MG 81 machine gun on some aircraft.

There was no Ju 88T-2, the final 'T' version to appear being the Ju 88T-3 which was based closely on the Ju 88S-3…even down to its powerplant, again with cameras rather than bombing equipment. With GM-1 boost, this version has been claimed to have been capable of 410mph (660km/h) at 27,887ft (8,500m). The Ju 88T-series retained the ability to carry stores on the single weapons station inboard of the engine nacelles, which characterised the Ju 88S, but for the carriage of long-range fuel tanks rather than bombs.

Long fuselage

The most radical of the recce Ju 88s was also one of the most unusual ⏩

This enigmatic machine might have been a one-off conversion, or one of the very mysterious Ju 88D-6 sub-types referred to in some post-war sources. It does, however, have Jumo inline engines as did the Ju 88T-3, rather than BMW 801 powerplants often quoted for the mysterious D-6. (via Peter Walter)

A very rare image of one of the few Ju 88H-1 aircraft, under inspection by Luftwaffe officers. This long-fuselage recce and patrol aircraft had FuG 200 Hohentwiel radar arrays attached to its nose.

departures from the basic design of the whole 'family', as decided originally in the programme's early days. Designed out of necessity during the war years, the Ju 88H series featured a considerably longer fuselage, to accommodate more fuel and thus to give the type genuine ultra-long-range capability and endurance. Built in small numbers, and in several distinct versions, the BMW 801-powered Ju 88H family was intended originally for long-range recce with armed maritime patrol as a useful addition, but in the event, some were intended for employment as the lower component of Mistel composites.

The initial requirement for this major conversion to the Ju 88 line came from the RLM during 1942, particularly for recce and long-endurance patrol work over the Atlantic. Junkers' designers identified the need for far greater internal fuel stowage, to allow for such extended-range operations. At that time, fuselage extension work was underway on the Ju 88G, and this concept was carried further for the Ju 88H. Basically, the fuselage was stretched both forward and aft of the wing, to avoid adversely affecting the type's centre of gravity. The resulting design also omitted the ventral gondola, and included an installation for up to three cameras in the stretched rear fuselage.

The first major version was the Ju 88H-1. This model featured FuG 200 Hohentwiel sea search radar, with prominent aerials attached to the nose/forward fuselage, underlining the

type's planned primary maritime patrol mission profile. Armament comprised two MG 81 machine guns in a pod beneath the fuselage offset to port, one of these 7.92mm weapons in the rear of the cockpit glazing, pointing aft (B-Stand), and optionally another windscreen-mounted example. The endurance was envisaged at approximately 12 hours; this would

have been very tiring for the aircrew, in the confined compartment characteristic of the whole Ju 88 family.

Somewhat optimistically, the Ju 88H-2 was planned as a zerstörer heavy fighter to combat Allied long-range maritime patrol aircraft, such as the Liberator and Sunderland. It had the radar and camera fit of the H-1 replaced by heavier armament of two MG 151/20 20mm cannons in the nose, and a battery of four more of these very effective weapons in a pod beneath the fuselage, offset to port.

These two versions were built in very small numbers at the Merseburg factory, but two further Ju 88H-series models existed, and both had further extended fuselages to house even more fuel. The Ju 88H-3 was intended as an ultra-long-range maritime patrol and recce aircraft similar to the H-1, and the Ju 88H-4 was to be similar to the H-2 in configuration and role. Both versions included enlarged tailplane surfaces as fitted to later models of the Ju 88G night fighter series, and were intended to be powered by Jumo 213 engines with methanol-water MW 50 boost.

Possibly false-coloured at the time (and not subsequently), this image shows a Ju 88D (possibly a D-2) believed to be coded 4U+GK of 2.(F)/123. Ahead of the cockpit sits the staffel emblem of 2.(F)/123, one of the principal exponents of recce Ju 88s.

Frontline service

In action right up to the final weeks of World War Two, recce Ju 88s pursued a lonely and often unsung career in Luftwaffe service. The type initially became operational in numbers during 1940, and continued to play an important part well into 1945. The exact total of Ju 88D-series aircraft has been the subject of considerable debate and disagreement among historians, with conflicting figures of 1,350 and 1,911 often being quoted.

Initial recce-configured Ju 88s that entered service during 1940 were either new-build or conversions of existing Ju 88A-1 and A-5 bombers. Designated A-1(F) and A-5(F) respectively, these aircraft pre-dated the dedicated recce Ju 88D series.

The Aufklärungsgruppe (reconnaissance group) was the basic Luftwaffe recce unit of the early war period. Many initial units were created up to the start of World War Two, but this expanded later due to wartime necessity. They were divided into short-range units and long-range groups…the latter being called a Fernaufklärungsgruppe ('Fern' meaning far or far distance). Most of the latter performed under Luftwaffe auspices, but a number worked specifically for Wehrmacht (army) planners under ObdH. Each Fernaufklärungsgruppe usually comprised individual squadrons named a staffel, their titles abbreviated so that, for example, the Fifth Staffel of Fernaufklärungsgruppe 122 was written 5.(F)/122. Those units supporting Luftwaffe operations were usually assigned directly to the Luftflotte for which they were providing information, each Luftflotte having at least one and often several more staffel assigned. Even so, this meant some units had a vast area of operations. The Junkers would always fly with defensive armament, and sometimes would carry bombs, depending on mission profile.

The Ju 88 eventually became the type of choice for long-range units, its speed and facility to defend itself unescorted, and its endurance (due especially to the ability to carry external long-range fuel tanks), were especially useful for wartime operations. In the event, Ju 88 recce units played an important part in all Luftwaffe operations from 1940 onwards. This included considerable participation in the Battle of Britain, followed later by operations in the Balkans, North Africa, Southern Europe and, crucially, over the Soviet Union. Data collected would be of vital importance to army and air force planners and intelligence personnel. The Ju 88's optical fit depended on ➤➤

Recce Ju 88s were operated by 5.(F)/122 on the Eastern Front during the winter of 1942-43, including this Ju 88D-1 F6+TN, with early production rudder hinge line. The vent for the petrol-fired camera bay heater is visible in the small fairing on the upper fuselage, above the cross.

Fitted with broad-chord VS 11 propeller blades (common to the Ju 88A-4, from which it was derived), this Ju 88D-1 4N+DK, of Aufklärungsgruppe 22, wore shabby winter camouflage for Eastern Front operations. Note the notched rudder hinge line of later production A-4/D-1 aircraft.

There were several 'oddball' one-off builds and proposed development lines associated with recce Ju 88s. This bizarre machine with BMW 801 radial engines, and four-bladed propeller units, is called a Ju 88D-7 by some researchers. (via Peter Walter)

the type of operation being flown, the heaviest camera being the Rb 75/30. Operations were usually flown at between 13,123ft to 19,685ft (4,000m to 6,000m), but later in the war as the performance of Allied fighters increased for interception, sorties were raised in altitude to 22,966ft (7,000m) or more.

In addition to daytime photographic work, techniques were developed for night photography. For this challenging task, flash bombs had to be carried (BLC 50A or 50B type). Modifications were made to the cameras to capture an image automatically, and keep the shutter open long enough to create a worthwhile negative – while also compensating for the speed and travel of the aircraft while the camera's shutter was open (cameras so configured carried an 'N' prefix). Ju 88s were used for this work in addition to Heinkel He 111s and other types, '88s being employed for night photography

particularly over Western Europe.

Weather recce was another role the Ju 88 performed through much of the war. The Luftwaffe formed several dedicated weather reconnaissance units, the title of which was Wettererkundungsstaffel (shortened to Wekusta or sometimes Westa). Usually, each Luftflotte had a Wekusta under its command, although several were subordinated directly to

the Oberkommando der Luftwaffe. Normally a Wekusta Ju 88 would carry a crew of four, with the weather observer being a specially trained member of the team; he would ideally be a meteorologist and, interestingly, some of these special observers were civilians with a 'paper' military rank. In addition to visual study, the aircraft itself would be fitted with various measuring instruments, for example to check wind speed; this data would be recorded on special onboard equipment, and if necessary the crew would make radio reports to their home base during the flight…especially if scouting ahead of an airborne bomber force.

Widespread operations

Among the initial Luftwaffe recipients of recce Ju 88s was Aufklärungsgruppe 122. This unit's 1st Staffel (1.(F)/122) is now generally regarded to have

A Ju 88D coded F6+DN of 5.(F)/122 in the freezing Russian climate. Narrow-chord VDM propellers suggest this is a Ju 88D-5, arguably the best of the actual D-series aircraft.

This Ju 88D-1 was operated by weather-recce unit Wekusta 1/ObdL during 1942. It was coded D7+LH. (via Peter Walter)

been the first to put the Ju 88D into service, several D-0 pre-production aircraft reaching the staffel in the summer of 1940. During the Battle of Britain, several squadrons had converted or were converting onto the Ju 88D (via a combination of D-0 and D-2 versions), including elements of Aufklärungsgruppe 120, together with 121, 122, and 123, while several were flying a mix of A-1(F) and A-5(F). One of the first, if not the first recce example of the Ju 88 to be lost over Britain was an A-1(F) of 1.(F)/121 on August 11, 1940; it was brought down by RAF Spitfires of 41 Squadron from RAF Catterick. By the end of the year the Ju 88D-1 was being readied for full-scale frontline service, particularly when sufficient supplies of the Jumo 211J engine started to become available for this model (and its bomber equivalent the Ju 88A-4), allowing the D-1 to supplant earlier recce models in 1941.

It was during the fighting over the Soviet Union from June 1941 onwards, and in North Africa, that recce Ju 88s proved indispensable. Luftflotte 4 over the Eastern Front had 3.(F)/121 as one of its main intelligence assets, other Eastern Front units including 3.(F)/10 and 3.(F)/33 (the latter later operating in the Mediterranean). Luftflotte 1 in the north and Baltic States used 5.(F)/122. For Mediterranean operations, important units included 1.(F) and 2.(F)/122, and 2.(F)/123, as well as Wekusta 26. Further north, 1.(F)/123 had a long association with the German-occupied Channel Islands, several of its Ju 88s coming to

grief at Jersey Airport. These included Ju 88A-1 WNr 0255 – presumably an A-1(F) – on November 3, 1940. On the Western Front, Luftflotte 3's activities also included 3.(F)/122's operations over Britain.

Construction of the recce Ju 88D series continued into 1944, but in the later stages of the war the type was replaced increasingly by the Ju 88T series. However, with the latter being much smaller in quantity, the Ju 88 recce force started to shrink considerably. This took place against the backdrop of the Germans withdrawing on all fronts. One of the first squadrons to employ the type was 1.(F)/121, by then operating for Luftflotte 3 later in 1943, for recce over British Channel ports. Among

The streamlined front and lack of lower fuselage gondola are noteworthy on this Ju 88T-1 coded 4U+VK of 2.(F)/123. It was photographed at Athens-Tatoi during the latter half of 1944. (via Peter Walter)

the later units to fly the Ju 88T was 2.(F)/123, stationed at one of the Athens airfields in Greece during the closing months of 1944.

Long-range flights

Ju 88H-1 long-fuselage recce and patrol aircraft played a brief part in the air war. The initial prototype/development aircraft, the Ju 88V89 (RG+RP, WNr 430820), first flew on November 2, 1943, powered by BMW 801ML radial engines. A second prototype/development aircraft followed, plus (it is now believed) eight production examples. After successful testing at Rechlin, the type entered service with the specialist 3.(F)/123 in France for ultra-long-range patrol and search missions over the Atlantic. This unit was already flying Ju 88Ds and had become proficient in long over-water recce flying. Relevant equipment for the Ju 88H-1 included FuG 200 Hohentwiel search radar and large underwing fuel tanks, to extend endurance. The first patrol began, according to the unit's official records, on May 3, 1944 from Rennes in western France. Flights of eight hours or more were accomplished in the following weeks, although it appears one of the aircraft was lost either to Allied action or an operational accident. Eventually, 3.(F)/123 re-equipped with the Ju 188 and that appeared to end the operational career of these big and impressive recce platforms. ◼

Adorned with the Comanche insignia of the 86th FS, USAAF, this Ju 88D-1 was surrendered by its Romanian pilot to the Allies during 1943. It was later flown to the US and still survives, as a prize exhibit in the National Museum of the United States Air Force. (USAAF)

UNDER NEW MANAGEMENT

Captured Ju 88s became a valuable source of technological knowledge for the Allies

Unsurprisingly, the Ju 88 was of great interest to British intelligence authorities.

As soon as crashed examples started to become available in quantity during 1940, an in-depth analysis of this very capable warplane could be made. Although this scrutiny started early in World War Two, the intelligence effort that surrounded the type eventually lasted to the final days of the war and beyond. Due to its nature as a multi-role type, all versions of the Ju 88 were deemed important technologically to the Allies. In the early war years this attention centred on bomber and reconnaissance versions of the Ju 88, but as the type became a very potent night fighter in the mid-war years, this tasking became the focus of considerable efforts by the British to see what made the type 'tick'… especially the radar black boxes of the increasingly sophisticated nocturnal fighters.

During the Battle of Britain, many shot-down Ju 88As littered southern England, although these were not as valuable as flyable examples. In the event, a small number of airworthy Ju 88s eventually fell into British hands and these proved very important. Even crashed examples yielded much useful information as far as structure and equipment was concerned. The 1940 edition of the famous British annual aviation review Janes' All The World's Aircraft (March 1941) devoted three whole pages to a description, accompanied by detail sketches of the Ju 88A-1's airframe and selected important parts.

Airworthy gems

Within the RAF, as far as captured and flyable Ju 88s were concerned, 1426 (Enemy Aircraft) Flight, nicknamed the 'Rafwaffe', was formed during 1941 to fly these aircraft and other Luftwaffe types, and demonstrate their characteristics to frontline units. The RAE facilities at Farnborough were utilised for some flight testing of captured German aircraft during the war, although certain types were of interest to other special units such as the Central Fighter Establishment. In

This interestingly camouflaged Ju 88S-1 coded RF+MT was captured at Villacoublay in France, during September 1944, and flew subsequently in Britain as TS472, including a period with 1426 Flight. (Malcolm V Lowe Collection)

A real prize for Allied intelligence was this Ju 88R-1 night fighter, which was landed at RAF Dyce by its defecting pilot on May 9, 1943. It is seen with its nose radar aerials removed, and with the British serial number PJ876. (John Batchelor Collection)

A common sight at war's end, large numbers of former Luftwaffe aircraft await scrapping. Here, several Ju 88s of various marks can be seen. If these aircraft still existed today, they would be priceless. (Malcolm V Lowe Collection)

those fighting against them in the front line. During a major public exhibition of captured German equipment, in Moscow during 1943, a Ju 88 was displayed prominently.

At the end of the war in Europe, Ju 88s were found strewn across former Luftwaffe bases all over Germany. This mainly included night fighters and heavy fighters, but significant numbers of bombers had also survived, and some in training units. Many night fighters were of continuing interest to the Allies, but in reality it was their black boxes that were actually of higher value. Nevertheless, eleven Ju 88s of differing marks were listed in contemporary documents as being newly assigned to the RAE Farnborough post-war. However, with the ending of hostilities, the threat posed by the Ju 88 was terminated, and virtually all Luftwaffe Ju 88 sub-types were surplus to requirements. The advent of jets, in any case, made the Ju 88 obsolete overnight, and most surviving airframes – even those used later for evaluation by the Allies – were scrapped unceremoniously. ▬

Although the Ju 88 airframe might not itself have been of great value any longer to Allied technical personnel at the end of the war in Europe, the Ju 388, with its pressurised crew area, was certainly of interest. This example was eventually test flown in the US as FE-4010. (via John Batchelor)

total, at least four Ju 88s are known to have flown with or been associated with 1426 Flight during its existence. These included a Ju 88A formerly of KGr 106 (allocated the British military serial number HM509, variously described as an A-5 or A-6); Ju 88A-5 of KG 30 which became EE205; Ju 88R-1 night fighter of NJG 3, later PJ876; and the Ju 88S-1, which became TS472. Of these, the Ju 88R-1 still survives, and is currently displayed at the RAF Museum, Cosford and features in the walk-around images of this book.

A second major survivor is the Ju 88D-1/Trop (WNr 430650) now displayed in the National Museum of the United States Air Force at Wright-Patterson AFB, Ohio. This aircraft (sometimes simply called a D-1) was formerly in Romanian service, and was surrendered to British forces during July 1943, before being passed to the USAAF.

Another Allied country that captured a significant number of Luftwaffe Ju 88s through combat was the Soviet Union. There is evidence that some flyable examples that fell into Soviet hands were actually put into service by the Russians, and this aspect is also referred to elsewhere in this publication. Actual evaluation by the Soviet authorities of the Ju 88 had started with the supply by Germany of at least one Ju 88 during 1940, before the two countries became enemies the following year. Later, several captured Ju 88s were evaluated at test establishments in the Soviet Union, where once again much valuable information was learned for

TESTING AND OTHER TASKS

Besides its main military roles, the Ju 88 was involved in various ancillary jobs, including test and trials work

Engine development work and research activity carried out in Germany was vital for the creation of a viable service-standard jet powerplant.

In Germany, as in Britain, the concept of the jet engine had been developed during the 1930s and into the 1940s, and the race was on in the Fatherland to ensure capable jet-powered combat aircraft were pressed into frontline service as soon as possible. The two most promising German designs were the BMW 003 and Jumo 004 turbojets; the latter was developed by the Ju 88's creator, and Ju 88s played an important role during separate test programmes for these two different engine types. This involved air testing the motors, for which an example was mounted on a special fitting beneath the Ju 88 test bed. Some of this trials work appears to have taken place at the E-stelle at

The Ju 88A-5 coded GH+FQ was used for testing of the Jumo 004 turbojet. The engine to be trialled in the air was carried on a special mounting beneath the aircraft's port wing centre section, replacing the normal bomb pylons/carriers. (John Batchelor Collection)

A rear view of Ju 88A-5, GH+FQ, employed by Junkers for Jumo 004 turbojet engine development. This project was successful, with the jet engine eventually entering service. (John Batchelor Collection)

Rechlin, and at other locations.

For airborne trials of the BMW 003, three Ju 88s were seconded to BMW's test establishment at Oranienburg, during early 1944. These are believed to have comprised two Ju 88A-5s and a Ju 88S. For air testing, one of the jet engines could be mounted on a special carrier beneath the Ju 88, the normal bomb pylons having been removed and replaced. It appears these trials, which involved civilian test pilots, were sufficiently successful for the BMW 003 to be cleared for further air testing in the aircraft type for which it was destined, the Heinkel He 162 austere jet fighter.

For air testing the Jumo 004, Junkers utilised a Ju 88A-5 coded GH+FQ, which flew successfully with the 11th test example, the 004V11. Although the development of the Jumo 004 was somewhat protracted, it was eventually

The Ju 88V19 was used as a development aircraft for the Ju 88C heavy fighter/zerstörer programme, for which it was re-named Z19. Here it sports an additional experimental MG 151/20 cannon mounted in the gondola, which was not used in service examples. (Malcolm V Lowe Collection)

88 development work and prototype testing. The trials explored increased armament, and the clearance of various munitions for use by operational units. Among these numerous trials was the testing of the LT 950D winged aerial torpedo, using Ju 88A-4 BF+YT at Gotenhafen (today's Gdynia in Poland). Trials of many other planned weapon systems and layouts were tried at the E-stelle at Tarnewitz on the Baltic coast, which specialised in weapons testing.

An unusual additional duty for a handful of Ju 88/188 versions was that

Typical of the many experimental Ju 88s was this airframe, SL+PC (sometimes called the Ju 88V60), which tested the extended lower fuselage intended for the Ju 88A-15…and which was later incorporated into the Ju 388's design. (Malcolm V Lowe Collection)

proved sufficiently to enter production and powered the Messerschmitt Me 262 jet fighter/fighter-bomber, and Arado Ar 234 jet bomber/reconnaissance aircraft.

Weapons trials

Several Ju 88s of various marks were seconded to official test centres, or to individual manufacturers, for trials work on such aspects as weapons development and proving (and propeller trials), while others remained with Junkers for further Ju

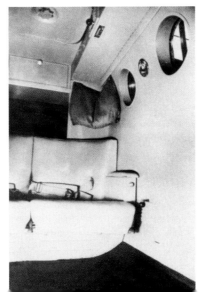

The fuselage interior and bomb bay of the Ju 88V7 was neatly converted into that of a smart transport and courier aircraft, for carrying passengers in this one-off arrangement. (Malcolm V Lowe Collection)

of passenger transport for high-ranking officials or company employees. One of the Ju 88s so converted was the Ju 88V7, used for a number of trials including development of the initial Ju 88A production series and Ju 88C-series, which entailed its nose being configured with the more streamlined 'solid' nose of that family. It also served as a high-speed communications aircraft, with its fuselage interior including the bomb bay specially converted with seating for up to four people.

FATHER AND SON

The Ju 88 became a vital component of the unusual Mistel composite aircraft programme, which was used in combat near the end of World War Two

One of the most dramatic participants in the exhibition of captured German aircraft at RAE Farnborough was this Mistel combination, sometimes called a Mistel S3A. (Key Collection)

Military necessity during times of war is often a fertile breeding ground for unusual or unconventional concepts.

Although Nazi Germany is often credited with being a source of many advanced aviation ideas, which in several cases is true, nevertheless some from the German aircraft industry and military during World War Two were more 'Heath Robinson' than practical reality.

Among the more bizarre, yet fascinating concepts that involved considerable development and trials time (for little practical gain) was the peculiar 'Mistel' (Mistletoe) composite aircraft project. This placed an operational, manned fighter above an unmanned explosives-equipped bomber, with the pilot of the fighter being expected to aim the bomber at a specific target…and then escape by

detaching his aircraft. This programme eventually reached operational status with the Luftwaffe, the bomber of choice being the Ju 88.

Historical precedent

Nazi Germany was not in fact the first country to explore this wacky concept. The idea of mounting one aircraft on top of another for separation in flight had existed in Britain during World War One, as a potential anti-Zeppelin defence, although little came of the plan at that time. It was Britain, though, that pursued the concept during the inter-war period. This involved the well-known and very successful civil Short-Mayo Composite, in which the flying boat S.21 'Maia' was the long-range mother ship for the smaller but similarly four-engined S.20 'Mercury' floatplane. The combination achieved a significant milestone during July 1938

by spanning the North Atlantic, when Mercury detached successfully in flight from Maia and flew on to Canada – at that time an important achievement. However, the outbreak of war in September 1939 ended this ambitious civilian endeavour.

Subsequently, by far the most development work on composite aircraft theory was performed in Nazi Germany. Unsurprisingly, from the outset this had a military rather than a civil purpose. Early concepts included the idea of a troop-carrying glider as the lower component, with a fighter as the upper portion of the combination, to allow the glider longer range than if it were towed conventionally. Featured was the DFS 230 troop-carrying glider, initially with a Klemm Kl 35 light aircraft on top, but later a Focke-Wulf Fw 56 and eventually a Messerschmitt Bf 109E fighter were used as the

the use of an unmanned explosives-filled bomber as the lower component, with a manned Bf 109 or Fw 190 as the upper part of the composite, the latter acting as a fighter/guidance aircraft. German reluctance – and later inability – to develop a viable long-range heavy bomber was an important reason why the composite aircraft gained momentum as a potential military programme.

It appears the concept was examined first with any great urgency by Junkers' test pilot Siegfried Holzbaur. However, the idea of an explosives-packed bomber as the lower component of a composite aircraft combination at first received little official interest. Nonetheless, as the war situation worsened for the Germans, and the need for long-range bomber operations against large targets mounted, the concept of an accurately aimed bomber filled with explosives gained increasing momentum. Junkers eventually formed a team of designers delegated specially to the creation of a viable composite. Much effort was duly made during the course of 1943, in conjunction with DFS and other interested parties; the original British experiments with composite aircraft concepts were also studied.

Basically, the required work involved comparatively straightforward (but nonetheless challenging) modifications of Ju 88 layout to accommodate a fighter mounted above. It included the

upper component. None of these combinations flew in combat, but they did prove the idea very effectively.

The thinking was crystallised around

addition of support struts to allow a Bf 109 to be mounted securely and safely above the bomber's fuselage, with the required mechanisms to allow it to detach in flight. Specially paired throttle controls and other necessary apparatus, such as linked fuel tankage and autopilot equipment, was also necessary, to allow the pilot of the Bf 109 to fly the whole resulting contraption. The composite would be flown to its target area by the pilot of the fighter, who would then release the unmanned bomber. The fighter had special joints with explosive bolts to ensure separation. Some form of primitive guidance was available with a Patin flight control system. After ➤➤

A close-up of the awkward strut-work needed to mount an Fw 190A above the fuselage of a Ju 88, in this case a combination thought to be a Mistel S2 at the end of the war. (Peter Walter Collection)

A training Mistel S1 during the latter half of 1944. In this case the upper component was possibly a Bf 109G, with the manned lower component a Ju 88C, proving that different versions of these types could be adapted for Mistel use. (all Malcolm V Lowe Collection unless stated)

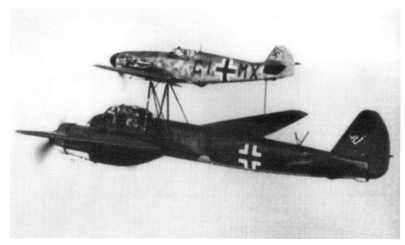

release the bomber would, theoretically, fly into its target under some form of autopilot guidance and explode, leaving the fighter free to return to base…or fight its way home.

Initial thinking centred on the use of the Ju 88A-series aircraft as being suitable for modification. Earlier Ju 88 bombers were by that time becoming surplus, so a potential pool was available for conversion. The forward fuselage of the Ju 88 was re-designed to be removable, with the normal nose containing the cockpit and standard flight controls being available for transfer flights with a human crew, but this could be removed easily and replaced by an unmanned warhead nose. Fitted with percussion 'crush' fuses and a shaped-charge warhead lined with soft metals, which

would create a molten plasma jet on detonation (intended to penetrate 'hard' targets such as a warship's hull), the warhead's main charge as fitted eventually was of some 3,748lb (1,700kg) of explosive and detonator.

Name game

The composite aircraft so created received a number of names in late-war Germany. The whole project went under the name of 'Mistel' (appropriate because the idea was something of a 'parasite' concept, just as Mistletoe grows on chosen trees). Many contemporary German documents call the composite aircraft 'Huckepack', and the terms 'Nero' and 'Vater und Sohn' (father and son) were also used. In English, the term 'piggy-back' (a translation of Huckepack) was used by

some US aircrew who encountered these contraptions in flight, while British parlance used 'pick-a-back'. A further German name or code was 'Beethoven-Gerät' or 'Beethoven device'.

The initial combination, called Mistel 1, married a Bf 109F (often an F-4, but other sub-types were possible) to a Ju 88A-4 (the Ju 88s so used commonly being 'recycled' examples). The exact date of the initial Mistel 1's first flight appears to be unknown, but during February 1944, official flight testing

was underway at the secret base of Peenemünde in northern Germany, where the concept was being proved as feasible. Training combinations were named Mistel S1. In the Mistel 2, however, the Bf 109 upper component

Flight testing in the Mistel programme took place at Ainring, southern Germany, and at Peenemünde in the north. The aircraft in this early Mistel combination are generally believed to be a Bf 109F-4 and Ju 88A-4.

A close-up of the Ju 88A/Fw 190A Mistel, often called a Mistel S3A, displayed in the exhibition of captured German aircraft at RAE Farnborough, during October and November 1945.

This Mistel 1 combination shows the Ju 88A lower component (probably a Ju 88A-4) fitted with the formidable-looking warhead nose of the operational composites. (Peter Walter Collection)

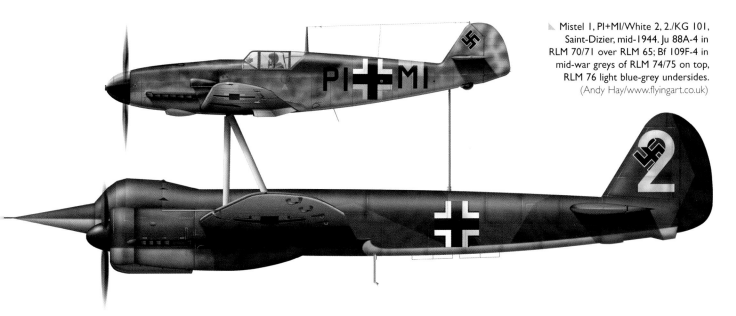

Mistel I, PI+MI/White 2, 2./KG 101,
Saint-Dizier, mid-1944. Ju 88A-4 in
RLM 70/71 over RLM 65; Bf 109F-4 in
mid-war greys of RLM 74/75 on top,
RLM 76 light blue-grey undersides.
(Andy Hay/www.flyingart.co.uk)

was replaced by the Fw 190 (usually but not always an Fw 190A-8). The type of Ju 88 lower component employed for this Mistel was, where possible, the later G-series; often new or little-used examples were employed.

Combat problems

The initial unit to deploy operationally with Mistel was a special staffel within the second gruppe of KG 101, later renamed as 2./KG 101. This unit began deploying to Saint-Dizier airfield in France, east of Paris, during June 1944. It was available to fly operations a little after the D-Day landings, but one of its Mistel 1s was shot down on June 14 by a Mosquito night fighter.

At first, Allied aircrew who encountered the Mistel in flight were perplexed as to what they'd found – but it soon became obvious that the

One of the few genuine Mistel 3 combinations completed, this composite (believed to be a Mistel S3C with a Ju 88G-10 lower component), was captured at the Junkers airfield of Bernburg during April 1945.

slow, lumbering composites were easy to shoot down. Nevertheless, 2./KG 101 did achieve partial success with its Mistel 1s. Several attacks were flown against Allied shipping off the Normandy coast, while it supported Allied forces after D-Day. It is possible a successful Mistel strike was made against the French battleship *Courbet*, which was being used as a partly sunk 'block ship' to create a sheltered area for Allied shipping, although the circumstances of this action remain contentious. However, the headquarters ship HMS *Nith* (K215) received a near-miss on the night of June 24 from what was believed to have been a Mistel, which damaged the ship seriously and killed several crew members.

Further sorties were flown from Saint-Dizier, with at least three Ju

88A lower components losing their way and crashing without purpose in England. Due to the bombing of Saint-Dizier airfield and the advance of Allied forces, KG 101's operations were duly cut short, having achieved little success.

Frontline Mistel use was concentrated later in the special operations bomber wing KG 200. Several staffeln within this wing's second gruppe eventually flew Mistel 2 composites, and were joined late in the war by elements of KG(J) 30 on the Eastern Front. A prize target for attack was identified by the Germans as the British naval base at Scapa Flow in Scotland. Code named Operation Drachenhöhle, the attack was planned for KG 200's Mistel 2 composites. However, while deploying to Tirstrup airfield in Denmark during February 1945, several KG 200 Mistels were discovered in flight by ▶▶

Bernburg airfield was captured by US forces in April 1945, and was the home to several Mistel-related aircraft. Included was the combination sometimes called a Mistel S3C (centre of the image), which is also illustrated elsewhere in this chapter. (Key Collection)

was negligible, and they did not prevent the eventual Soviet victory in the East.

During their brief time on the front line, the Mistel achieved very little and was easy prey for Allied fighters while in flight. Its attacks on D-Day shipping from June 1944, and against Soviet targets on the River Oder in the final stage of the war, were potentially of the greatest military value, but these unorthodox contraptions often proved to be of greater danger to their operators than to the enemy.

Future projects

Additional to the Mistel combinations that actually existed, further Mistel projects were under development or being devised by Germany late in World War Two. These included

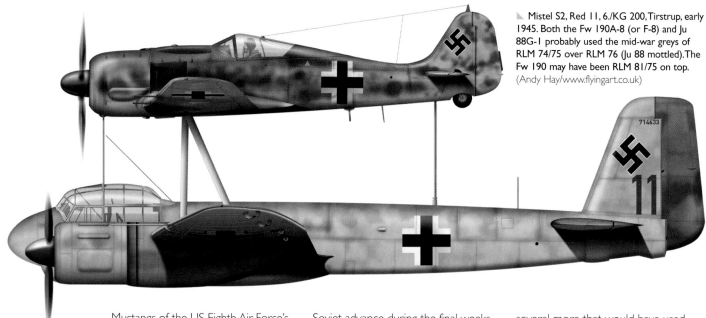

Mistel S2, Red 11, 6./KG 200, Tirstrup, early 1945. Both the Fw 190A-8 (or F-8) and Ju 88G-1 probably used the mid-war greys of RLM 74/75 over RLM 76 (Ju 88 mottled). The Fw 190 may have been RLM 81/75 on top. (Andy Hay/www.flyingart.co.uk)

Mustangs of the US Eighth Air Force's 55th Fighter Group, which shot them all down. Further, a visit to Tirstrup by RAF Mosquito fighter-bombers of the Fighter Experimental Flight, based at Ford in Sussex, did more damage to already-arrived Ju 88/Fw 190 combinations, and the Scapa Flow attack never took place.

Late war Mistel operations were aimed primarily against Soviet forces and installations. This included the intended Operation Eisenhammer (Iron Hammer), a proposed attack during February or March 1945 on Soviet electrical power and hydro-electric targets – which was prevented by the rapid advance of Soviet forces. A last-ditch series of sorties was flown against various Soviet bridgeheads and bridges, to try to slow the relentless

Soviet advance during the final weeks of the war in Europe. Although some actual Mistel bridge attacks did indeed take place, their overall military value

several more that would have used the Ju 88 as the lower component, although others were intended for different lower elements. Several proposed Ju 88 designs went under the general name Mistel 3. Among them was a very long-range composite known as the Führungsmaschine, which would have used the long-fuselage Ju 88H-4 as its lower component with an Fw 190A-8 above. The extended fuselage of the Ju 88H-4 housed extra fuel, and this Mistel was intended as a long-range pathfinder; the Fw 190 (which had its own extra fuel) acting as an escort fighter for the Ju 88 once detached if the Mistel was attacked by enemy fighters. None of these planned late-war Mistel projects was ever used operationally, as far as is known.

A dramatic gun camera image showing a Mistel 2 combination of KG 200 under attack at low level, with a crew member baling out. It was being pursued by Lt Bernard Howes of the 55th FG. (USAAF)

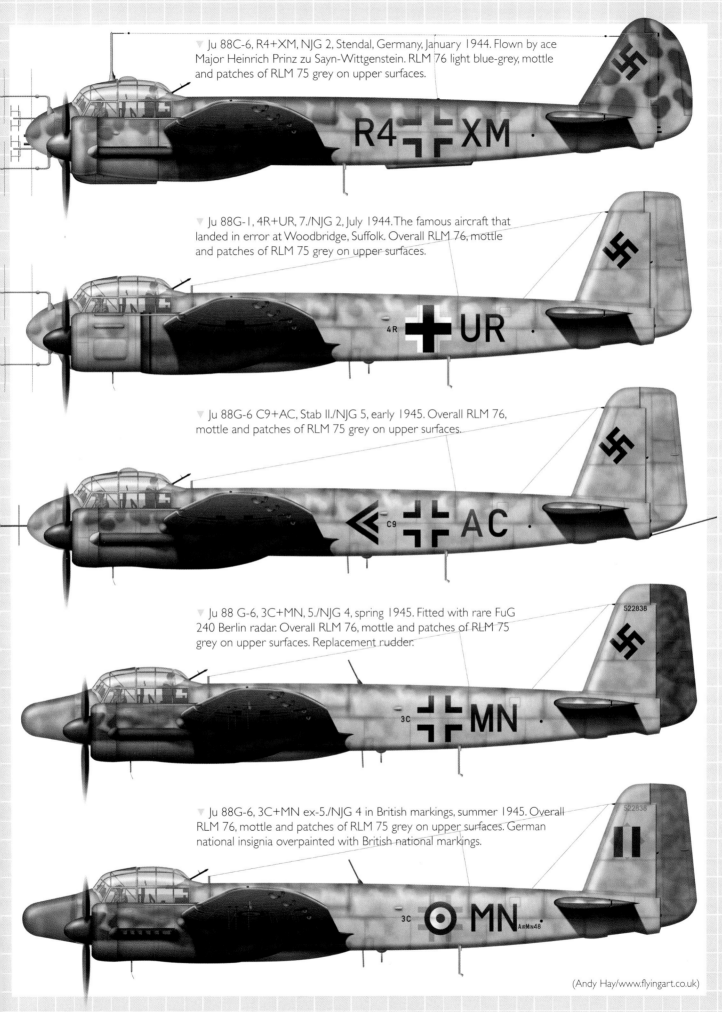

▼ Ju 88C-6, R4+XM, NJG 2, Stendal, Germany, January 1944. Flown by ace Major Heinrich Prinz zu Sayn-Wittgenstein. RLM 76 light blue-grey, mottle and patches of RLM 75 grey on upper surfaces.

▼ Ju 88G-1, 4R+UR, 7./NJG 2, July 1944. The famous aircraft that landed in error at Woodbridge, Suffolk. Overall RLM 76, mottle and patches of RLM 75 grey on upper surfaces.

▼ Ju 88G-6 C9+AC, Stab II./NJG 5, early 1945. Overall RLM 76, mottle and patches of RLM 75 grey on upper surfaces.

▼ Ju 88 G-6, 3C+MN, 5./NJG 4, spring 1945. Fitted with rare FuG 240 Berlin radar. Overall RLM 76, mottle and patches of RLM 75 grey on upper surfaces. Replacement rudder.

▼ Ju 88G-6, 3C+MN ex-5./NJG 4 in British markings, summer 1945. Overall RLM 76, mottle and patches of RLM 75 grey on upper surfaces. German national insignia overpainted with British national markings.

(Andy Hay/www.flyingart.co.uk)

EXPORT EMPLOYMENT

In addition to its widespread German service, the Ju 88 flew
in combat with a small number of foreign operators, and
even continued in 'overseas' service after 1945

Finland was
an important
export
customer of the
Ju 88A. This very
smart example,
Ju 88A-4
JK-267, was
photographed
in an image
dated May 1943
at Onttola, the
home of LeLv
44. (all via John
Batchelor unless
stated)

The Ju 88 was of such great
importance to the Luftwaffe,
the type was not widely
supplied to Germany's allies.
Nevertheless, some did serve with
other countries in a combat role, albeit
in comparatively small numbers.

Finnish success

One of the most accomplished and
arguably best-known of the 'export'
operators of the Ju 88 was Finland.
This country had to survive a major
invasion by the Soviet Union in the
Winter War, which began during late

1939, and duly fought on the side
of Nazi Germany in the so-called
Continuation War. To that end, the
Finns were supplied with considerable
German munitions, although some
Allied equipment also found its way to
the Finnish armed forces. During 1943
the hard-pressed Finnish government
agreed to the purchase of 24 Ju 88s,
all being the A-4 version (sometimes
called Ju 88A-4/R). Finnish air and
groundcrew were duly based at Tutow
in Germany to receive instruction on
the type, and the first aircraft were
handed over during April 1943.

One of the aircraft crashed during
delivery, killing the crew, leaving the
Finns with 23 examples (numbered
JK-251 to JK-273). The intended unit for
these aircraft was Lentolaivue 44 (LeLv
44), based at Onttola. This unit was a
former Bristol Blenheim operator, and
it eventually comprised four flights with
four Junkers each. It flew its first Ju 88
sorties during May 1943, and was in
action against a major Soviet offensive
that September, forward based at Utti.
Finland eventually removed dive brakes
and limited diving, due to concerns
over airframe stress. The Finns duly

This LeLv 44 Ju
88A-4, JK-260,
came to grief
in a rather
expensive
landing,
wrecking the
aircraft. The
Finnish national
insignia had no
connection to
the Swastika
carried on the
vertical tail
of Luftwaffe
aircraft.

fought hard against overwhelming odds into 1944, with the Ju 88s in the thick of the action, but had to sign an armistice during September 1944… and subsequently turned against their former German allies. During that time the unit changed its title to PLeLv 44, the final wartime sortie being made in April 1945 by JK-268, by which time the operating unit was PLeLv 43. Post-war, the Ju 88 remained in Finnish service, albeit in dwindling numbers until the later 1940s, JK-271 being retired during 1948.

French service

By far the most significant operator of the Ju 88 aside from the Luftwaffe was, somewhat ironically, France. This country was not just forced to participate in repairing damaged Ju 88s for the Luftwaffe following the country's capitulation, but ironically, France also became an operator of the type in 1944 in combat against the Germans. Junkers persisted in French service even after World War Two.

From 1941 onwards, several French factories had been assigned to the refurbishment of Luftwaffe Ju 88s. These included the Clichy and Argenteuil establishments of SNCASE and a Breguet factory in Biarritz. Commencing during 1943, the workshops of SNCASE in Toulouse, southern France, also became involved in this programme.

Following the liberation of Toulouse in August 1944, several Ju 88s that had been damaged by USAAF bombing were rebuilt in the factory of Saint-Martin-du-Touch, specifically for use by the French against their former German occupiers. This was accomplished by gathering spare parts and engines that were to be found in many locations in southern France. The first reconditioned aircraft for French service was received very rapidly, on September 16, 1944 by the celebrated Colonel Dor. Deliveries subsequently continued at the rate of two aircraft per month until May 1945. They formed part of the nucleus of a French Forces of the Interior unit, called Groupe Dor. During December 1944 this somewhat mercenary organisation was integrated into the recently reconstituted Armée de l'Air, with a new designation - Groupe de Bombardement (GB) I/31 'Aunis' (this is sometimes written as 1/31 due to a changeover of French unit titling).

Further 'new' Ju 88s subsequently joined the Armée de l'Air. From March 1945, added to the aircraft already by then delivered from Toulouse were the first six aircraft repaired by the AAB (Ateliers Aéronautiques de **⟫**

Loaded and ready to go, this Finnish Ju 88A-4 of LeLv 44 has its crew entrance hatch at the end of the lower fuselage gondola open, to allow crew escape in the event of problems before take-off.

A Finnish Ju 88A-4 of LeLv 44 being prepared for a bombing mission. Finland eventually removed the dive brakes from its Ju 88s, and limited diving to avoid airframe stress… therefore lengthening airframe life.

▶ An apparently re-touched but nonetheless interesting image of a Finnish Ju 88A-4 over water, bearing that country's roundels as well as former German crosses on its wings. Finland's Ju 88s retained their Luftwaffe splinter camouflage pattern.

▼ The French flew the Ju 88A in combat against the Germans, via a mixed bag of repaired and reconditioned aircraft, firstly with the FFI-associated Groupe Dor, then with the Armée de l'Air's GB I/31 'Aunis'. Some of the aircraft concerned wore unique spotted camouflage. (Malcolm V Lowe Collection)

Boulogne) factory, and the workshops of Clichy and Argenteuil.

As far as combat was concerned, Groupe Dor was engaged in operations from on (or around) October 16, 1944 attacking the German positions of the Pointe de Grave and Royan (the well-known 'Royan Pocket'), first from Toulouse, then from Cazaux. These operations continued until the end of hostilities in May 1945, the unit by then having become GB I/31, some German forces continuing to resist until the final days of the war. Bombing missions consisted of attacks in small groups of three to ten aircraft, loaded with former German munitions, the level attacks comprising a simultaneous release of bombs by all the Junkers involved; the French called this 'American bombing'. During the campaign, GB I/31 suffered comparatively heavy losses due to accidents, caused by such factors as engine failure and lack of pilot proficiency; some aircrew had not been allowed by the Germans to fly for a number of years. Several airframes were thus destroyed in accidents, while two were shot down by anti-aircraft fire.

The conclusion of World War Two was not the end of the story of the French Junkers. Ju 88 reconditioning in fact continued at SNCASE factories at the rate of three aircraft per month until 1947, by which time more than 80 examples had been repaired (possibly some were 'new build' examples constructed from spares). They were mainly Ju 88A bombers, but some were zerstörer C-6s, and there was at least one R-1 fighter. Five Ju 188s were reconditioned for service with the recently reconstituted French naval aviation (Aéronautique Navale). Post-war, the only operational unit of the Armée de l'Air to use the Ju 88A

was GB I/81. During 1946 this outfit was stationed in Tunisia for aerial policing duties. The unit's surviving aircraft were eventually assigned to the Centre d'Expériences Aériennes Militaires at Mont-de-Marsan, southern France, where they served as test-beds for various weapons trials. Some were also stationed at Cazaux for wide-ranging experimental work until the early 1950s. At least one aircraft was employed as a test-bed for jet engine research and trials.

Naval operations

The French Aéronautique Navale (sometimes written as Aéronavale) operated a mixture of various marks of Ju 88 and Ju 188. At least five '88s were taken on charge by the Aéronautique Navale for service in a new trials unit, the Section d'Essais de l'Aéronautique Navale, which was formed on December 19, 1944. This organisation later became Escadrille de Servitude 10S during July 1945, units such as this in the Aéronautique Navale usually being tasked with second-line trials, training or reserve duties. Among the five original aircraft taken on charge, one was a Ju 88A-17 torpedo bomber, and three others (WNr 144539, 144502 and 144219) were Ju 88A-14s. Escadrille 10S subsequently had the type on its books until the final examples were retired officially in 1951, added to by at least one and possibly more Ju 188Es. One of the most important tasks carried out by the Junkers of this unit was a series of torpedo trials, involving torpedoes known to the French as the L50 and T114. Some of these trials

were carried out in the vacinity of Saint-Tropez on the coast of southern France, with the Junkers based at Luc.

German allies

Among other principal exponents of the Ju 88 in combat during World War Two was Hungary, which was closely allied to Germany and flew them alongside Luftwaffe units, against Soviet forces. The exact number of Ju 88s supplied to Hungary, or had associations with Hungarian operations, has been open to considerable debate. However, recent work by that country's historians suggest as many as 91 Ju 88s of several marks were used by Hungarian units… or were at least available for Hungarian operations. This included mainly Ju 88A-4 and A-14 bombers, and Ju 88D recce aircraft. A rare Ju 88C heavy

fighter was also included.

In Hungarian service, Ju 88 bombers flew in various frontline units, including the 3/1 Bombázó század (Bomber Squadron) and the 4/1 Bombázó század (the latter known as the Boszorkány – 'Witch' Bomber Squadron). Recce examples were flown by the 1/1 Távolfelderítő század (Long Range Reconnaissance Squadron). There is a well-known sequence of photographs taken during 1943, of an aircraft of the latter unit numbered F.9+14 being refuelled; the 'F' of the aircraft's code/serial standing for Felderítő (Reconnaissance).

Romania was another employer of the Ju 88 in the war against the Soviet Union. Most Ju 88s supplied to Romania by the Germans were A-series bombers, but also included were several recce-configured ⏩

although some of the latter were simply used for spares. Spain continued to fly the Ju 88 post-war, but unlike other German types did not put the Junkers into local production.

Another German ally that flew the Ju 88 was Italy. In this case, however, the aircraft supplied by Germany were mainly veteran Ju 88As (many of which had seen better days), one Italian historian describing them as 'worn out'. It is possible that around 50 or 52 Ju 88s were supplied for Regia Aeronautica service, mostly A-4 bombers, although some recce examples were apparently among those aircraft received. The dilapidated state of several examples meant they were relegated to training duties at Forli airfield, and it's possible a number were grounded altogether. Any plans to put them into widespread frontline service were, in any case, scuppered with the dramatic events in Italy following the Allied landings, and the toppling of Mussolini during July 1943. That effectively ended interest in the type as a frontline bomber for the Regia Aeronautica.

Although not a Ju 88 operator, Switzerland became the recipient of a Ju 88A-4, which wore (albeit briefly), Swiss national markings. The aircraft

aircraft. Among them was the Ju 88D-1/Trop WNr 430650 now displayed in the National Museum of the United States Air Force, at Wright-Patterson AFB, Ohio. This aircraft (sometimes simply called a D-1) was surrendered to British forces during July 1943, before being handed subsequently to the USAAF.

The least known of all Ju 88 operators is Spain. This country was officially neutral during World War Two, but was linked closely to the Axis powers through its Fascist dictator Franco, and Spain benefited

substantially from German military aid. This included the provision of aircraft types such as the Ju 88 and Messerschmitt Bf 109. During 1943, Spain purchased ten second-hand Ju 88A-4 bombers from Germany. At least some of these were delivered from the Toulouse workshops in France, where Ju 88s were refurbished under the German occupation. They were assigned to 13 Regimiento, based in Albacete (Los Llanos), and supplemented by some 13 further ex-Luftwaffe examples interned after landing in Spain for various reasons;

concerned, was a Ju 88A-4 from I./ KG 54 coded B3+MH, which landed at Dübendorf airfield in Switzerland during October 1943. It subsequently wore Swiss markings for a time.

Russian diversion

In a further twist of irony in the story of non-German Ju 88s, the first genuine export to a foreign power was the supply of at least one example to the Soviet Union. Although Nazi Germany and the Soviet Union became mortal enemies following the German offensive Operation Barbarossa, which began on June 22, 1941; prior to that time the two countries were allies – at least on a diplomatic level. During August 1939 Nazi Germany and the Soviet Union had signed a so-called non-aggression pact – the famous Molotov-

Ribbentrop agreement – often described as the Nazi-Soviet Pact. A spin-off of this apparently friendly liaison was the supply to the Soviet Union of several types of German warplanes; among them was a Ju 88. Identified as a Ju 88A-1 WNr 088050 (known for export as a Ju 88K-1), it wore the German civil registration D-AXVM and was delivered during 1940. It was tested thoroughly by the Soviet aviation authorities, and many sources state this was the only Ju 88 willingly supplied to the Soviet Union by the Germans.

The story becomes complicated at this point, though, due to claims that the Soviet Union obtained more than one example of the Ju 88 at that time. Some historians have asserted that one of the batch of Ju 88A-0 aircraft with four-bladed propellers, registered

WL+008, also made its way to the Soviet Union, where it was examined by the trials and test organisations LII and NII VVS.

During the conflict between Germany and the Soviet Union, a comparatively large number of Ju 88s of different marks fell into Soviet hands. This was hardly surprising due to the number of airframes shot down, or which forced-landed. There is evidence that flyable examples that fell into Soviet hands were actually put into service by the Russians, but just how many of these were used in combat by the Soviets – if any – remains a subject that requires further research. An intact and apparently potentially airworthy Ju 88A was displayed at a major exhibition of captured German equipment, held in Moscow during mid-1943. ▄

A number of captured Ju 88s flew with British markings. This ex-KGr 106 Ju 88A-5 received the British military serial HM509. Behind it is Airspeed Oxford Mk.II V3781.

Mystery surrounds this very early Ju 88 with four-bladed propellers, registered WL+008, which several writers have claimed was supplied to the Soviet Union. (Malcolm V Lowe Collection)

Loading a Ju 188A-2 of I./KG 6, probably for an operation against a British target. The very prominent barrel of the flexible-mounted 20mm MG 151/20 cannon protrudes from the 'glasshouse' nose structure in the type's A-Stand position. (all Malcolm V Lowe Collection unless stated)

TRIPLE-DIGIT WONDERS

Early in the development of the Ju 88, Junkers formulated alternative layouts that eventually resulted in a new but closely related derivative, the Ju 188

When Junkers initially created plans for Ju 85 and Ju 88 proposals during 1936, which were duly submitted to the Reichsluftfahrtministerium (RLM), appended to the initial design layouts were additional thoughts that eventually led to a wholly new bomber programme.

These ideas centred on major changes to the nose and cockpit contours, introducing neatly streamlined and continuously curved cockpit glazing. This would replace the planned conventional stepped nose, with its windscreen separate to what became known as the 'beetle eye' or 'beetle's eye' forward glazing employed eventually on the Ju 88A bomber series. These streamlined formats proved too radical for the RLM's more conservative staff, and in any case, there was no real need for this design at the time because the layout that became the Ju 88A production standard seemed practical enough without changes being necessary.

However, the idea of the continuous fully glazed nose contours persisted in the thinking of Junkers' designers, particularly as it offered potentially increased performance due, in part, to its low-drag shape. This, coupled with the use of Jumo 213 bomber engines offering greater performance than the Jumo 211 standardised for the Ju 88A series, led to renewed interest from the RLM...and the go-ahead for limited development. In characteristic fashion, this interest almost at once turned into incomprehensible demands for large-scale production, with unrealistic deadlines that could not possibly be met.

Nevertheless, Junkers carried on regardless, drawing some features from the previous Ju 85B programme,

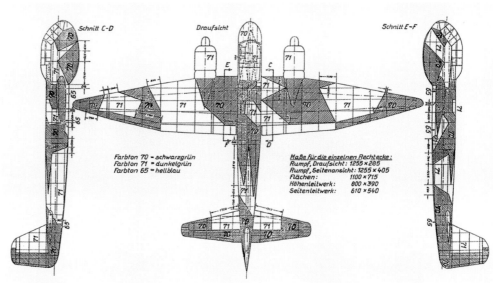

A Junkers drawing dated August 1942, showing the 'Muster B' splinter camouflage pattern for the Ju 188 (with BMW engines shown), which remained relevant during subsequent manufacture. The shades were two greens on top (RLM 70 Schwarzgrün and 71 Dunkelgrün), and light blue underneath (RLM 65 Hellblau). (via John Batchelor)

and during June 1940 the first prototype/development aircraft of the proposed Ju 88B series took to the air. It was the Ju 88V23. Powered originally by Jumo 211B engines due to scarce availability of the 213 powerplant, Jumo 213A engines were fitted retrospectively, but eventually the entire Ju 88B series standardised on the BMW 801 radial engine as its basic powerplant. At first Junkers had thought of the BMW 139 as another possible alternative to the Jumo 213, but the BMW 801 (as also used in several other marks of Ju 88) eventually became accepted.

In the event, just ten Ju 88B airframes were built. They are sometimes called Ju 88B-0, but in reality, most if not all bore Versuchs numbers denoting their true role as experimental/development airframes. They were numbered from the Ju 88V23

onwards, apparently in sequence to Ju 88V32. Armament planned for the Ju 88B, which was originally intended as a bomber version, was a twin MG 81Z 7.92mm machine gun installation in the A-, B- and C-Stand positions. However, some of these aircraft were unarmed and others just partly armed. A zerstörer version was envisaged, but like all other imagined Ju 88B versions, it was never series produced.

Instead, development work was pursued on a related bomber project, the Ju 88E. This, and the related Ju 88F recce aircraft, was also not built on the production line, but was a direct link to the major development series that did attain considerable manufacture and frontline combat employment, the Ju 188.

Limited operations

The small number of Ju 88B Versuchs aircraft had varied careers, but some did reach combat. Most were used for various development issues and spent much time with Junkers on trials work, and at the E-Stelle Rechlin on test and evaluation duties. Several, though, were employed as fast, high-altitude recce platforms, some on clandestine long-range flights over ostensibly ⟫

The Ju 88V27 was one of the ten Ju 88B prototype/development airframes, and was used in several trials programmes, some of which led to the Ju 188. Note the turret in the upper cockpit glazing, similar to that used on the Ju 188. (Junkers)

The Ju 88V44/
Ju 188V1
coded NF+KQ
featured in
a series of
Junkers' publicity
photographs,
to demonstrate
the new Ju 188
layout. It was
the original
prototype/
development
aircraft for the
whole '188
series.

friendly territory. It is believed these
aircraft were flown unarmed, their
high-level flight profile making them
less vulnerable to interception. Just
what the camera fit was in each
aircraft is still a mystery, but it appears
that no two examples were alike.
Principal operating units were the
Versuchsstelle für Höhenflüge or
VfH, sometimes called Kommando

Rowehl, and at one point the 3./
Aufklärungsgruppe ObdL. Several
Ju 88B airframes are known to have
flown with this unit, sometimes over
the Soviet Union. The Ju 88V26
was apparently shot down by the
Russians on one of these sorties.
1./Aufklärungsgruppe ObdL also
operated the type, the Ju 88V31 being
recorded as damaged in a crash at

Aalborg, Denmark, during March 1943
while with this unit of the Luftwaffe's
high command.

Necessary maturation

Although not series manufactured, the
Ju 88B and E layouts offered potential
gains in performance over the existing
'Anton' design, whose production was
in top gear during 1941. As explained

The Ju 88B
pioneered many
changes to
the standard
Ju 88A layout,
included later in
the production
Ju 188
configuration.
It is believed
this is the Ju
88V24, the
second of the Ju
88B prototype/
development
aircraft.

This Ju 188E is either a very early production E-1 model, or a pre-production example. Echoing several very early Ju 188E bombers, it had dive brakes fitted beneath its wings...a feature that was later omitted entirely from production Ju 188s.

earlier, the Ju 88A series was becoming outclassed by Allied aircraft during 1942, and a line of development commenced to improve the design that led, in the short-term, to the Ju 88S family. However, for the long-term a more significant development programme was called for, and that duly evolved as the Ju 188.

In the event, some 'B' airframes participated in the new Ju 188 tactical light/medium bomber programme. Important among these was the Ju 88V27, which was tested with one of the new type's distinctive features, a small turret on top of the cockpit canopy structure, containing a 13mm MG 131 machine gun. The Ju 88V27 in effect had acted as a prototype/ development aircraft for the Ju 88E project. Other changes adopted for the production-standard Ju 188 aircraft were an increase in wingspan over the Ju 88A-4 of around 6½ft (2m), giving a wingspan of 72ft 2¼ in (22m).

A significant change from the previous Ju 88 line was the adoption of the Jumo 213 inline engine, replacing the established and reliable Jumo 211, which powered so many previous versions. The Jumo 213 was developed specifically as a bomber engine, although later it powered the high-altitude Focke-Wulf Ta 152 single-engine fighter. In its 213A-series form, this engine could produce 1,730hp for take-off, and was installed in the Ju 188 in the same fashion as in the Ju 88A series, with an annular radiator at the front of the engine cowling;

this gave the incorrect impression from the front that it was a radial unit. Installation and pipework for the Ju 188 had to be redesigned compared to the Jumo 211 of the Ju 88A series, however, due to the different capacity and cooling needs of the Jumo 213. In general, the latter was a considerable improvement over the earlier 211. It had a pressurised cooling system that required considerably less cooling fluid, which allowed the engine to be smaller and lighter, and several improvements to achieve higher RPM. These changes

boosted power by more than 500hp under certain operating conditions. As an alternative, however, the trusty BMW 801 radial engine was also made available for the Ju 188.

Significantly, an alteration was made to the tail surfaces, which were enlarged compared to those sported by 'Anton' airframes. This was an important change that also affected the production of the Ju 88G night fighter series, as explained earlier in this book. Pioneering work on the new configuration was made with the ❷❯

A Jumo 213A-powered Ju 188A-2 of KG 6 (one source claims KG 66) runs up its engines during the summer of 1944. Note the open crew entry hatch in the lower fuselage, which would not be closed until the last minute in case speedy exit was required.

▶ Pointed wing tips, redesigned forward lower fuselage and altered vertical tail of the Ju 188 series, compared to the Ju 88, are well represented in this view of Ju 88V44/Ju 188V1, NF+KQ. (John Batchelor Collection)

▼ A very early production Ju 188E-1, or a pre-production example, sits among several Junkers Ju 53/3m transports. The streamlined forward fuselage/cockpit glazing of the Ju 188 was very different from the 'beetle's eye' of the Ju 88A.

Ju 88V44 prototype/development airframe, which was in effect the prototype for the Ju 188 series. To that effect it was later re-designated as the Ju 188V1, and was joined eventually by three other prototype/development aircraft specifically for the Ju 188 programme.

Major versions

The Ju 188 was series manufactured in four main versions and these were the Ju 188A/E bombers, and Ju 188D/F recce aircraft.

Initial production centred on the BMW-powered Ju 188E series. A pre-production batch of 12 examples was completed and delivered from

February 1943. They are often called Ju 188E-0 in published sources, but it now appears there was no real 'Null' series; instead, the pre-production batch was a mix of early production-standard aircraft. The first series production sub-type was the Ju 188E-1, the powerplant of this model being standardised on versions of the BMW 801, the 801D-2 model offering 1,700hp for take-off.

The Ju 188A-series was powered by the Jumo 213A-series, the A-1 sub-type being the initial production version following the Ju 188E-1 in terms of deliveries. During production in late 1943, the Jumo became available in a new MW 50 methanol-water

injection-boosted version. This gave an excellent 2,200hp for take-off. With this engine fitted, the designation changed to Ju 188A-2, and deliveries commenced in earnest during the early part of 1944.

Bomber versions of the Ju 188 were able to carry a weapons load of up to 6,614lb (3,000kg). Armament consisted of a flexible-mounted 20mm MG 151/20 cannon in a new A-Stand position (in the forward streamlined glazing), a new B1-Stand with flexible-mounted 13mm MG 131 machine gun in the rear of the cockpit glazing, and a new B2-Stand featuring the new HDL 131 hydraulically operated turret in the roof of the cockpit glazing structure…

also containing an MG 131. The lower forward fuselage gondola of the Ju 88A was gone altogether, because the changes to the front fuselage did not stop at the new streamlined nose contours, the lower fuselage shape also being redesigned considerably. There was, however, still a rearwards-firing C-Stand gun position with a flexible mounting, for weapons such as the twin MG 81Z 7.92mm machine gun. Several Ju 188A-2 airframes featured a revised turret, which was armed with an MG 151/20 cannon, with a single MG 131 machine gun in an altered C-Stand position.

Sea search and torpedo attack were important capabilities of the Ju 88A series, and these were retained in the Ju 188. Although the FuG 200 Hohentwiel radar normally required a substantial set of aerials to be attached to the forward part of the fuselage around the nose, a modified version mounting a small, low-UHF-band FuG 200 sea-search radar set was nose-mounted for the Ju 188E-2. The standard external underwing bomb carriers/pylons inboard of the engine nacelles were removed, and in their place (in similar fashion to the Ju 88A-17) was fitted one special PVC carrier for a torpedo, the type most often associated with this version being the LT F5b of 1,653lb (750kg).

The Jumo-powered equivalent was the Ju 188A-3.

Following the bomber versions of the Ju 188, the two recce models came into their own during 1944, when Germany's need for higher-performance surveillance platforms was more acute. The basic bomber configuration was modified with the removal of the bomb aiming equipment and forward defensive armament, and a camera installation similar to that of the Ju 88D series was made available – although again the camera fit required depended on the particular mission profile. The standard high-altitude Rb 75/30 camera was thus of most importance. Additional fuel cells were added in the bomb bay to extend the range to a creditable ⏩

A wrecked Ju 188A photographed in Belgium following its capture by Allied forces. It had formerly been operated by I./KG 6 with the unit code 3E+PH. (via John Batchelor)

The Ju 188G was a planned bomber version with a deepened fuselage, which would have included a manned rear turret for a small gunner, seen here on the Ju 188V2 WNr 260151. It did not enter production.

With a hangar disguised as a house in the background, this Ju 188E-1 was captured by Allied forces at an airfield probably in Denmark. It had apparently flown with KG 66 and wore the unusual polka-dot camouflage sometimes used on late-war Luftwaffe bombers.

2,113 miles (3,400km), and echoing exactly the Ju 88D series, long-range fuel tanks could be carried externally. The Ju 188D-1 was otherwise very similar to the A-1; the D-2 was to receive FuG 200 Hohentwiel nose radar for naval search and recce. There were parallel recce conversions of the Ju 188E series, designated Ju 188F-1 and F-2.

Planned developments

In addition to series-production Ju 188A/E bombers and Ju 188D/F recce versions, several other re-worked examples of the basic Ju 188 layout were envisaged but not manufactured

in quantity. Alphabetically, the first was the Ju 188C, which would have been armed with a power-operated, remotely controlled FA 15 turret in the end of the fuselage, containing two MG 131 machine guns, aimed via a rearwards-looking periscope in the cockpit roof glazing. This version did not proceed, and neither did the Ju 188R. The latter would have been a radar-equipped night fighter with MG 151/20 or 30mm MK 103 cannons in its nose. During 1944, three Ju 188E were modified to this configuration but the extensive glazing of the Ju 188's cockpit and forward fuselage was not conducive to night fighting,

due to glare, and the type did not show performance gains over any existing night fighters, resulting in abandonment of the concept.

Similarly, the Ju 188G and 188H were not taken further. These versions for bombing and recce would have had a deepened fuselage to allow for a greater internal bomb load, or for the recce versions a similarly deepened body would have allowed more room for cameras and extra fuel. In a strange twist, the envisaged deepened fuselage appeared to present the possibility to mount a manned gun turret in the tail. A miniature garden gnome would have been needed

Oslo-Gardermoen in Norway was a major base for Luftwaffe operations. This impressive array of Ju 188A-3 torpedo bombers was photographed after the German surrender of May 1945, the aircraft having been flown by III./KG 26. (via John Batchelor)

to climb into such a small space, and these versions were not pursued.

Also envisaged for the Ju 188 family was a series of specific high-altitude versions, which were planned to be pressurised. They were designated as the Ju 188J heavy fighter, Ju 188K bomber, and the Ju 188L recce version. The latter two were intended to carry their loads in a long pannier under the central fuselage, reminiscent of the development work carried out with the Ju 88A-15. A Ju 188S fighter and Ju 188T intruder were also considered. Before any of these diverse planned versions were developed properly, they underwent a change of designation through the RLM to Ju 388, reflecting the fact they were markedly different compared to standard production Ju 188 bombers and recce aircraft.

Luftwaffe service

The Ju 188 had a comparatively brief but nonetheless generally successful period of service with the Luftwaffe, which was cut short by the worsening war situation and growing emphasis on defensive fighter, rather than bomber missions, which even meant some bomber units of the Luftwaffe converted hastily into makeshift fighter

organisations. The exact number of Ju 188s built is yet another subject that has troubled historians. Figures of 1,076 and 1,234 have been used widely…a problem of accurately determining the correct total being missing and conflicting documentation, especially where production records from Junkers and its sub-contractors do not appear to match aircraft taken on charge in the official military Quartermaster General's summaries.

Bomber Ju 188 airframes found their way to a handful of operating units, such as KG 6 and KG 66, while recce-configured '188s operated with several

of the Aufklärungsgruppe units already established on the Ju 88D. This service was nowhere near as widespread in comparison with the major operational career of the Ju 88A/D.

During mid-1943, several early pre-production or early production Ju 188s joined the trials and evaluation unit, Erprobungskommando 188. In autumn 1943 the type joined I./KG 66, a unit that specialised in using the Ju 188E as a pathfinder, while operating from Montdidier for the bombing of Britain during the winter of 1943-44. A further early operator of the type was I./KG 6, equipped previously with ⏩

Several fully serviceable Ju 188A-3 torpedo bombers of III./KG 26 at Oslo-Gardermoen, following the end of hostilities in May 1945. The nearest aircraft is fitted with FuG 200 Hohentwiel radar aerials on its nose. (via John Batchelor)

The nose of a KG 26 Ju 188A-3 equipped with FuG 200 Hohentwiel search radar, for maritime work. It is believed to have been coded 1H+FR. The oval fairing with its flat transparent panel beneath the nose was for the bomb aimer's Lotfe bomb sight on Ju 188 bombers.

Looking somewhat out of place with British roundels over its rather elaborate late-war Luftwaffe camouflage, this Ju 188A-3 coded 1H+GT, formerly of III./KG 26, was surrendered to the British at Lübeck following a flight from the Courland Pocket. It was later transferred to Britain with the Air Ministry number AM 113.

the Ju 88S and stationed in Brétigny and Melun-Villaroche during the summer of 1944.

Ju 188s therefore participated in the concluding Baedeker raids and during Operation Steinbock in the first half of 1944, followed by action to combat the Allied landings in Normandy on and after June 6 of that year; this included bombing raids and mining operations in the English Channel. This was alongside Ju 88s of various marks, as explained earlier. In operations over England, it was found necessary to fit a device to the nose glazing structure of Ju 188 bombers that had been vital earlier in the war for Ju 88s bombing British targets – the so-called 'Kuto-Nase' for cutting the cables of barrage balloons.

A force of Ju 88s and Ju 188s were involved in what became the last major raid on London by conventional aircraft during the night of April 18-19, 1944. According to Luftwaffe records, of the attacking force of 125 aircraft, around just half were effective. Thirteen of the bombers were lost, including a Ju 188E believed to be of KG 2 'Holzhammer', which was credited to a Mosquito of 85 Squadron, RAF. At the time, KG 2 was a Dornier Do 217 unit transitioning to the Ju 188.

The torpedo bombing specialist KG 26 also operated the Ju 188. Due to its specialised nature, this unit survived until the end of World War Two. It has come to light recently that some of the last flights by Luftwaffe aircraft

during the conflict were made by this unit, via a mix of Ju 88A and Ju 188A torpedo bombers to evacuate trapped German 'tourists' (soldiers) from the Courland Pocket, Latvia, where they were encircled by Soviet forces. The aircraft landed on May 8 at Lübeck-Blankensee airfield. At the end of the war in Europe during May 1945, many of this unit's other Ju 188A-3s were surrendered to Allied forces at various airfields in Norway, notably Oslo-Gardermoen. Those at the latter were destroyed later by Allied specialists.

Last gasp

Arguably the most impressive of the Ju 88 line (and its related developments) was the Ju 388. This potentially excellent, high-altitude bomber,

With its beautifully rounded, pressurised nose section, the Ju 388 certainly looked streamlined and advanced. This aircraft, KS+TA, was one of the few bomber Ju 388K-0 pre-production aircraft, but lacked the planned remote-controlled tail gun installation.

The Ju 388V8 WNr 300002 (coded PG+YB) acted as a prototype/development aircraft for the Ju 388L-0 recce aircraft. The longer cowling housing the turbo equipment for the BMW 801 powerplant is seen clearly in this view.

fighter/bomber destroyer and recce aircraft was the ultimate iteration of the original Ju 88 design, and had World War Two continued it would have been a very useful asset to the Luftwaffe. As it was, the appearance of the type in limited manufacture came too late to make any difference whatsoever to its outcome. Nonetheless, it was an advanced design with the then-pioneering system of pressurisation.

Junkers had been interested in the concept of pressurisation for some time prior to the start of World War Two. The company was therefore in a good position to place this – at the time – very challenging concept into production. As explained earlier in this chapter, Junkers had intended to produce pressurised versions of the Ju 188 family, and in their developed form those concepts became the Ju 388 series.

The new aircraft was intended to be manufactured with the same designation letters as the three original Ju 188 experimental versions from which it originated: the Ju 188J, K, and L. The Ju 388J model was planned as a high-altitude fighter, to counter the perceived threat of possible Boeing B-29 Superfortress raids on Germany. These did not materialise, but the intended fighter would have been armed with two MK 103 and two MG 151/20 cannon in a solid nose, similar to that of the Ju 88C-series, for employment as a daylight bomber destroyer. For night fighting, the MK 103s would have been replaced by smaller and lighter 30mm MK 108 cannons, while a second pair of dorsal-mounted, upward-firing MK 108s were planned in the mid-fuselage (Schräge Musik) installation similar to that of the Ju 88G night fighter. Radar envisaged for the nocturnal version was the FuG

218 Neptun with the Hirschgeweih forward fuselage antenna array. Wingspan was intended to be 72ft 2 ¼in (22m).

The Ju 388K was to be the high-altitude bomber version of the '388 line, with a deepened and thus enlarged bomb bay. This concept had already been examined for and pioneered by the Ju 88A-15. The Ju 388L recce model would have had cameras mounted in this deepened fuselage structure, together with additional fuel tanks for high-altitude, long-range missions. Available for the latter models would have been a power-operated, remotely controlled turret in the end of the fuselage containing two MG 131 machine guns mounted one above the other, aimed via a rearwards-looking periscope in the cockpit roof. This new fitting gave a potentially excellent field of fire, obviating the need for rearwards- ➠

The elegant Ju 388L pressurised recce aircraft was produced in small numbers. This Merseburg-manufactured Ju 388L-0 was coded DW+YY and had the WNr 300291.

A close-up of the nose of one of the very rare Ju 388K-1 bombers, with RT+KD behind it, probably photographed at Junkers' main factory at Dessau. Note the turbocharged BMW 801 engine installation with its lengthened nacelle (the turbo was positioned behind the engine, and exhausted at the top).

bomber Ju 88s. The provision of increased-size tail surfaces, in the style of some Ju 88/188 models, was a major improvement.

A batch of further prototype/ development aircraft was built, but engine problems, especially the protracted difficulties with the Jumo 222, caused considerable delays. It also became clear the feared USAAF B-29 bombers were being delivered to units based in China and the Pacific for operations against the Japanese, and would not be operating over Germany in the immediate future. This caused a major shift of emphasis in the whole Ju 388 programme, with bomber and recce versions duly receiving most emphasis. Indeed, it was eventually the recce-configured Ju 388L-series that gained most development time, due to the growing need for a recce platform able to fly at high altitudes, and evade the increasingly efficient Allied defences.

The exact number of Ju 388s of all types finally built has been the subject of considerable debate following the war. German records are incomplete, and Allied forces discovered part-built, damaged and destroyed airframes at different locations in Germany. It is possible that more than 40 Ju 388L-1s with BMW 801 power were completed, plus smaller numbers of the Ju 388K and an even lesser total of the fighter Ju 388J. Almost all were powered by BMW 801 powerplants. Important in the production process were ATG and Weserflug. Several post-war German sources have suggested that approximately 20 Ju 388L-0 pre-production examples and 60-plus Ju 388L-1s were completed. Partial testing was carried out at Rechlin and initial appraisals by Luftwaffe aircrew were very positive, although in reality many 'bugs' needed to be ironed out before the type could have entered full-scale frontline service.

One impressive survivor of the Ju 388 line exists, a Ju 388L-1 WNr 560049, completed in 1945. The Ju 388 with its pressurised crew area was certainly of interest to the Americans at the end of the war, and this surviving example was evaluated in the US post-war as FE-4010. It was built by Weserflug, and is currently stored at the National Air and Space Museum in the US.

firing, hand-held machine guns in the B-Stand and C-Stand positions… allowing deletion of the lower fuselage gondola of earlier Ju 88s.

Powerplant problems

Somewhat optimistically, three sub-types of each of the three versions were envisaged, comprising three different engine types. The Ju 388L-1, for example, was intended for BMW 801J power (sometimes called BMW 801TJ), an advanced turbocharged version of the basic BMW 801 radial much-used in the Ju 88 family; the Ju 388L-2 would need the highly complicated, advanced but challenging 2,500hp Jumo 222A/B (opposite rotation) or supercharged 222E/F 24-cylinder liquid-cooled engines; the Ju 388L-3 would employ the

supercharged Jumo 213E. In the event, the Jumo 222 proved troublesome in development, and therefore the only powerplants used for the Ju 388s built were the BMW 801 and Jumo 213 series, almost all being of the former.

Development of the Ju 388 was challenging, with Junkers already fully stretched on Ju 88 and Ju 188 work, and distracted by the disastrous Ju 288 programme. The general war situation was, in addition, starting to deteriorate seriously for the Germans. The initial prototype/development airframe, the Ju 388L-0/V7, contained many Ju 188 components. It first flew on December 22, 1943. Junkers' designers were pleasantly surprised by the new aircraft's flying characteristics, especially at high altitude, which were markedly better than previous

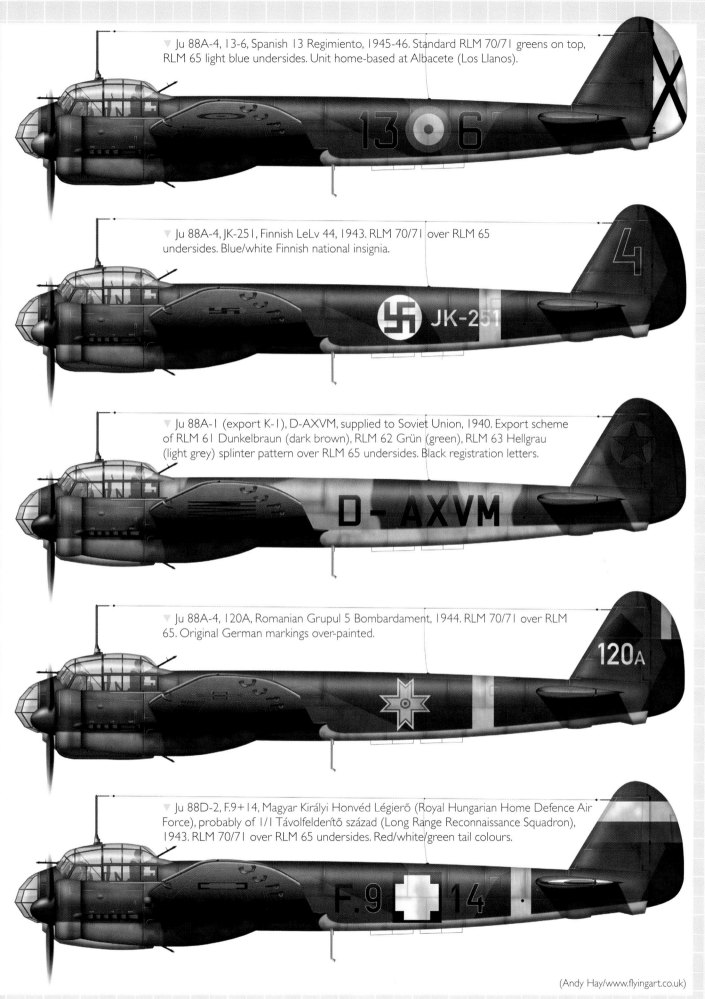

▽ Ju 88A-4, 13-6, Spanish 13 Regimiento, 1945-46. Standard RLM 70/71 greens on top, RLM 65 light blue undersides. Unit home-based at Albacete (Los Llanos).

▽ Ju 88A-4, JK-251, Finnish LeLv 44, 1943. RLM 70/71 over RLM 65 undersides. Blue/white Finnish national insignia.

▽ Ju 88A-1 (export K-1), D-AXVM, supplied to Soviet Union, 1940. Export scheme of RLM 61 Dunkelbraun (dark brown), RLM 62 Grün (green), RLM 63 Hellgrau (light grey) splinter pattern over RLM 65 undersides. Black registration letters.

▽ Ju 88A-4, 120A, Romanian Grupul 5 Bombardament, 1944. RLM 70/71 over RLM 65. Original German markings over-painted.

▽ Ju 88D-2, F.9+14, Magyar Királyi Honvéd Légierő (Royal Hungarian Home Defence Air Force), probably of 1/1 Távolfelderítő század (Long Range Reconnaissance Squadron), 1943. RLM 70/71 over RLM 65 undersides. Red/white/green tail colours.

(Andy Hay/www.flyingart.co.uk)

DESPERATE MEASURES

Two potentially important derivatives of the Ju 88, the Ju 288 and Ju 488, never reached series production…and for significant reasons

W hen the development of the Ju 88 was in progress, thought was already being given by Junkers (and separately by the RLM) as to a potentially more capable successor. An obvious expression of this was the development of the Ju 188, but Junkers additionally devised several more complicated but related schemes, which kept the company's design offices busy into the latter stages of World War Two.

Complicated disaster

An early line of thought at Junkers was a more powerful twin-engined Ju 88 look-alike, with most of its bomb load stowed internally, and able to fly at greater heights. This was made possible partly by the proposed advent of more powerful engines, and the continuing research into pressurisation. As noted earlier in this book, Hugo Junkers had become interested in the concept of pressurisation for high-altitude flight

prior to the Nazis' accession to power, and this was research that the Junkers company pursued during the 1930s – originally with the Ju 49 of 1931, and later the EF 61 of 1935-1937.

The new bomber project was numbered by Junkers as the EF 73, and later by the RLM as the Ju 288. It was intended to be state-of-the-art, and was promoted enthusiastically to the RLM and Nazi hierarchy by Junkers' Dr Heinrich Koppenberg. Among its advanced features were unmanned, low-drag remote-controlled turrets to cut the number of crew, and to allow all personnel to be positioned in the bulbous pressurised forward fuselage. Essentially, the RLM wrote a specification, the famous 'Bomber B' project, around the planned aircraft. Other companies were allowed to compete for this requirement, and did so with the Focke-Wulf Fw 191, Henschel Hs 130, and other designs which did not progress; although Junkers was in reality the winner before the process had even started. 'Bomber A' was the troubled Heinkel He 177 Greif (Griffin).

Unfortunately for Junkers, the Ju 288 proved to be a disaster. Development

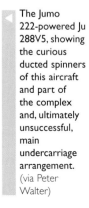

Providing an interesting comparison, this image shows the Ju 288V2 bearing the civil registration D-ABWP, parked beside the Ju 88V16 D-ACAR. The Ju 288V2 was BMW 801-powered, and had measuring instruments in its temporary nose probe. (Malcolm V Lowe Collection)

The Jumo 222-powered Ju 288V5, showing the curious ducted spinners of this aircraft and part of the complex and, ultimately unsuccessful, main undercarriage arrangement. (via Peter Walter)

of the Ju 288's planned engine, the advanced but challenging Junkers Jumo 222, was difficult. As the design of the aircraft itself matured it grew in complexity, size and, alarmingly, its weight increased considerably. A noted failing of the Ju 288 layout was its complicated and ultimately unsuccessful main undercarriage arrangement, which proved calamitous for the few Ju 288s built. The type's two-wheel, over-engineered main undercarriage units were very complex in their retraction cycle and prone to collapse, and were one of the many reasons why the Ju 288 never came near to series production.

The initial Ju 288, Ju 288V1, first flew during early 1941 (some sources claim November 1940). Problems with the Jumo 222 engine resulted in early Ju 288s being powered by the well-established BMW 801 radial engine. Several Ju 88s were used in the Ju 288 development programme, including the Ju 88V2 and V5, and the original Ju 88V1, fitted with a pressurised forward fuselage structure. The first Ju 288 to fly with the Jumo 222 was the Ju 288V5, but the planned Ju 288A bomber series

inventory was problematic for the Germans, and belatedly the Ju 88 was studied in detail during 1944 by Junkers as a possible basis. It would have been a rival to such programmes as Heinkel's He 277, a part of the abortive 'Amerika Bomber' thinking. Junkers planned to create a simplified (therefore presumably easy to manufacture) design by combining sub-assemblies or other parts of the Ju 88/188/288/388, with a new wing centre box and mid-section fuselage components. Production aircraft were to be powered by the troublesome Jumo 222 engine, and a wingspan of just less

than 102ft 8in (31.29m) was envisaged. Manufacture of six prototype/development examples (Ju 488V401 to Ju 488V406) was desired and at least some manufacture commenced. Major components of the first two were entrusted to Latécoère at Toulouse in France. During the night of July 16-17, 1944, French saboteurs bravely entered the Latécoère factory and blew up significant parts of the airframes. The Ju 488 project never recovered from this setback and the concept, echoing so many German bomber programmes, was terminated, in this case during November 1944. ▬

The DB 606-powered Ju 288V11 was used on development work to perfect the troublesome main undercarriage arrangement planned for the Ju 288 series. It is seen here during 1942, while performing this function. (via Peter Walter)

was scrapped eventually, in favour of the redesigned four-crew Ju 288B, which itself was terminated. The altered Ju 288C, powered by the Daimler Benz DB 606 or 610 engines, also failed to reach series manufacture. In total, 22 Ju 288 prototype/development aircraft are known to have been built, the Ju 288V1 to V14, and the V101 to V108. At least one of these, the Ju 288V9, apparently survived into 1945 on engine trials work.

Long-range bomber
The most significant related development of the Ju 88 layout would have been an ambitious, four-engined, long-range strategic bomber. The lack of such an aircraft in the Luftwaffe's

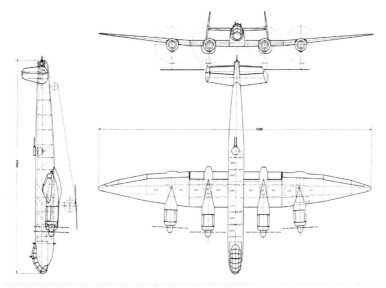

The Ju 288 was ungainly even in flight. Jumo 222-powered Ju 288V9 VE+QP seen here displays the twin fin and rudder layout, and bulbous pressurised crew compartment planned for the Ju 288 series. (Junkers)

A Junkers diagram of the planned Ju 488 layout, confirming the proposed wingspan of 31.29m. (Malcolm V Lowe Collection)

RISING STARS

French aircraft industry.

A colourful character in the Junkers line-up at Dessau was Brunolf Baade. A former member of the Bayerische Flugzeugwerke AG (later Messerschmitt AG) and the US aircraft industry, Baade joined Junkers in 1936 and became important in the company's design organisation, being involved in project management for the development of the Ju 88/188, including the Ju 88B programme.

Like many Dessau employees, Baade found himself in the Soviet-controlled sector of Germany after World War Two ended. In Cold War East Germany, he rose to prominence with a project that is still little-known in the West, which aimed to create an indigenous jet-powered airliner. As the Baade 152 airliner project, the new aircraft bore his name. In the event, just three of these advanced and futuristic-looking jet airliners were constructed, of which two actually flew, with the first example being involved in a fatal crash during March 1959. The programme was scrapped, though, when East Germany became fully subject to accepting Soviet-built airliner types.

Two emerging luminaries of the aviation industry sat among Junkers' ranks…

A significant personality in the design of both the Ju 87 Stuka and Ju 88 - and thence the Ju 188 - was Prof Dr-Ing Heinrich Hertel.

It is somewhat surprising that Hertel does not normally receive more credit nowadays for the design of the latter two types. A gifted aeronautical engineer with several major diplomas and a professorship, Hertel worked for Heinkel before moving to Junkers prior to the war starting. Essentially, he became Junkers' head of aircraft development, working closely with Ernst Zindel and others in the company's technical team at Dessau, and as such oversaw design work on the Ju 88 and Ju 188. Like many of Junkers' 'top brass' in the technical team, he survived World War Two, and, ironically, worked in the post-war

Brunolf Baade (right) is seen with other important members of the Junkers technical team - Ernst Zindel (second from left) and Paul Kratz (left) on the shop floor at Dessau, conversing with an elderly factory worker. (via Peter Walter)

Heinrich Hertel (right) and Brunolf Baade, both of whom were important to Junkers' wartime programmes… and were involved in Ju 88 and Ju 188 development. (via Peter Walter)

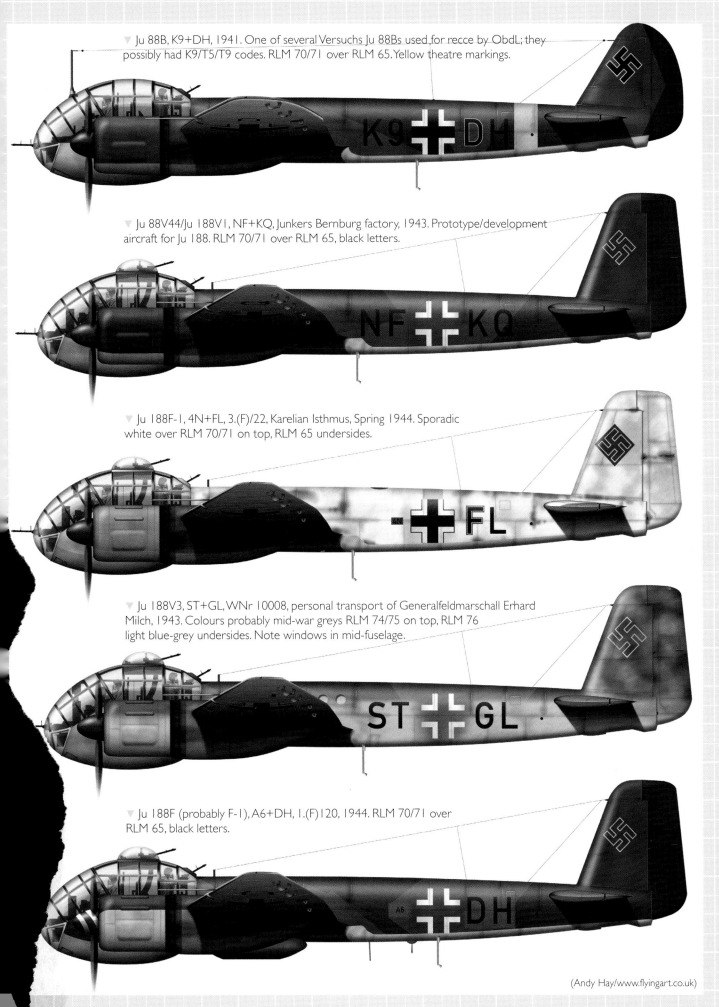

▼ Ju 88B, K9+DH, 1941. One of several Versuchs Ju 88Bs used for recce by ObdL; they possibly had K9/T5/T9 codes. RLM 70/71 over RLM 65. Yellow theatre markings.

▼ Ju 88V44/Ju 188V1, NF+KQ, Junkers Bernburg factory, 1943. Prototype/development aircraft for Ju 188. RLM 70/71 over RLM 65, black letters.

▼ Ju 188F-1, 4N+FL, 3.(F)/22, Karelian Isthmus, Spring 1944. Sporadic white over RLM 70/71 on top, RLM 65 undersides.

▼ Ju 188V3, ST+GL, WNr 10008, personal transport of Generalfeldmarschall Erhard Milch, 1943. Colours probably mid-war greys RLM 74/75 on top, RLM 76 light blue-grey undersides. Note windows in mid-fuselage.

▼ Ju 188F (probably F-1), A6+DH, 1.(F)120, 1944. RLM 70/71 over RLM 65, black letters.

(Andy Hay/www.flyingart.co.uk)

KITOGRAPHY

This modelling listings section does not feature every Ju 88 family product, but is rather a selection of representative items. Most have been gleaned from the websites of Hannants (www.hannants.co.uk) and Scalemates (www.scalemates.com). Besides the products listed here, more can be found on both websites. Kit manufacturer names are abbreviated as follows:

Bilek (Bil), Cyberhobby (Cyb), Dragon (Dra), Hasegawa (Has), Hobby Boss (HB), Hobbycraft (HOB), Italeri (Ital), Revell (Rev), Monogram (Mon), Special Hobby (SH), Zvezda (Zve).

KITS

1/72

Airfix
A03007 Ju 88A-4

AMT/Ertl
8897 Ju 88G-1/G-6
8898 Ju 88C-4/C-6

AMtech
729201 Ju 88S-1/T-1

729203 Ju 88S-3/T-3
729206 Ju 88H-3 Mistel 4 and H-4 Fuhrungsmachine

Hasegawa
00830 Ju 88G-1 'Night Fighter'
00852 Ju 88C-6 'Nachtjagdgeschwader'
00867 Ju 88A-11 'North Africa'
00885 Ju 88R-2
00920 Ju 88D-1
00939 Ju 88A-4 'Finnish Air Force'
00963 Ju 88A-6/U 'KG 54'
01555 Ju 88A-4
01562 Ju 88G-6 'Nachtjäger'
01916 Ju 88G-6 'Berlin Radar'
01932 Ju 88A-14 'Geismann'
01955 Ju 88G-6 'Schoenert'
01975 Fw 190A-8 & Ju 88G-1 'Mistel S2'
01999 Ju 88A-8 w/Ballon Cable Cutters
02016 Ju 88S-1/S-3 'KG 66'
02037 Ju 88C-6 'Nightfighter'
02073 Ju 88T-1
02113 Fw 190A-8 & Ju 88G-1 'Mistel 2'
02137 Ju 88C-6 'Hunter Killer'

Junkers Ju88C-6 'HUNTER KILLER'

02245 Ju 88C-6 'Zerstörer'
Hobby Boss
80297 Ju 88 Fighter
Italeri
117 Junkers Ju 188A-1/E-1
018 Ju 88A-4
022 Ju 88C-6
038 'Torpedobomber' Ju 88A-17

072 Ju 88A-4 and Bf 109F Mistel 1
1287 Ju 88A-4 (upgraded tooling)
Kora
72018 Ju 88G-10 Mistel S3C (Fw 190 not inc)
72021 Ju 88S-1
72022 Ju 88S-2
72023 Ju 88S-3
72057 Ju 88G-7
72075 Ju 488V-401
LF Models
7230 Ju 88V28 (B-1)
Revell
04130 Ju 88A-4/D-1
04672 Ju 88A-4 Bomber

04856 Ju 88C-6 Z/N
Zvezda
7269 Ju 88G-6
7282 Ju 88A-4
7284 Ju 88A-17/A-5
1/48
Cyberhobby
5563 Ju 88G-6 Nachtjäger and Luftwaffe Pilots
5565 Ju 88A-4 Schnellbomber and Luftwaffe Groundcrew
Dragon
5509 Ju 88G-6 Nachtjäger
5510 Mistel 2/S-2
5513 Ju 88A-6 Balloon Cutter

5521 Ju 88G-1/G-10
5528 Ju 88A-4 Schnellbomber
5536 Ju 88C-6 Zerstörer

5540 Ju 88C-6 Nightfighter
5543 Ju 88P-1 w/75mm Pak 40
Hasegawa
07440 Ju 88A-10 (ICM tooling)
07446 Ju 88A-5 Eastern Front
Hobbycraft
HC1601 Ju 88A-4
HC1605 Ju 88C
HC1606 Ju 88G
HC1607 Ju 88S
ICM
48232 Ju 88A-5
48233 Ju 88A-4
48234 Ju 88A-14
48235 Ju 88A-11
48236 Ju 88A-4/Torp

Monogram-Promodeler
5970 Ju 88C-6
5948 Ju 88A-4
Planet Models
059 Ju 388
078 Ju 388V2 (J-0) 'Störtebel
222 Ju 388J-3 'Jumo 213 eng
Revell
03935 Junkers Ju 88A-4 (ICM